POTIPHAR'S WIFE

And Other Poems

Ballantyne Press
BALLANTYNE, HANSON AND CO.
EDINBURGH AND LONDON

POTIPHAR'S WIFE

AND OTHER POEMS

BY

SIR EDWIN ARNOLD

AUTHOR OF "THE LIGHT OF ASIA," "LIGHT OF THE WORLD," ETC.

LONDON

LONGMANS, GREEN, AND CO.

1892

CONTENTS.

—⋅⊷⋅—

Egyptian Poems.

Japanese Poems.

Other Poems.

Egyptian Poems.

POTIPHAR'S WIFE.

(After the versions of the Koran, and the Persian poet Jâmi.)

I.

In Memphis, underneath the palms of Nile.
  The Lady Asenath a house did build
For love of Hebrew Yûsuf; who, erewhile
  With flame unquenchable her breast had filled :
The treasures of Prince Itfîr 'stablished it
A summer-palace for her fancies fit.

II.

White, in the blue Egyptian sky, it soared
  With mighty graven stones reared outwardly ;
This side the gate—enthroned—sate Horus, Lord,
  Finger to lip ; and, on that other, Thmei,
Mother of Truth, holding her asp and wand,
Glared with great granite face across the land.

3

III.

Inwardly, by an alley of black shade,

 The footstep passed on checkered slabs set square,

Into a walled court; where a colonnade

 Framed a glad garden full of odours rare

From heavy blooms and fruits.　Without was seen

Golden Noon flaming, here 'twas Evening green!

IV.

And all the wall was painted movingly

 With high-wrought lore, and solemn-storied things:

Anubis, herding souls, was there to see,

 And Thoth the Judge: and proud-apparelled kings

Driving to wars, and bringing spoil again,

Their chariot-wheels rose-red with blood of slain.

V

And elsewhere Heaven was shown, with bliss unbroken,

 Whereto those mild immortal sisters lead,

Isis and Nepthys; and, for certain token,

   Scarabs in holy rows.   The limner's reed

Had drawn their foreclaws holding emblems three

Of Life, and Changelessness, and Sanctity.

VI.

And, elsewhere, frowned Amenti—Hell :—but over

   The silver plumes swayed, teaching how the Dead

Should pass beyond dire Typhon, and discover

   Paths to the happy Light, where Ra's bright head

Rebukes all darkness, Regent of the Sun ;

And Phtah, Kneph, Athor—every Sacred One.

VII.

Also, that cloistered walk was compassed in

   With pillars wonderful for work and hue :

This one a palm-stem ; that papyrus thin ;

   Yonder, in stone, lotuses pink and blue.

And from the garden and the colonnade

A roofed way to the inner rooms was laid.

VIII.

For inner chambers were there seven :—each fashioned
    With matchless wit to make each goodlier
Than that last seen.   So, heart and eye, impassioned
    Unto the inmost passed, devised by her,
High Asenath, for love's deep hiding-place,
Beautiful, marvellous, all peace and grace.

IX.

Through latticed loops Nile's cooling ripple came—
    Musical, lulling,—to that dim retreat
Which had for light one silver lamp's faint flame
    Burning with fragrant oils before the feet
Of Pasht, in speckled stone, Pasht with cat's head,
And long arms on her levelled knees outspread.

X.

The forty carven columns round about
    Showed each some masterpiece of subtle craft :

A musk-deer here, in river-reeds, breathes out

   The very musk-scent from him : there, a waft

Of bulrush-heads to the quick current bend,

And the slow crocodiles to dry land wend

XI.

Sunning wet scales.   And, next, a grey fox watched—

   In syenite—doves on a tamarisk-tree

Done out of green rock.   Wings and necks were matched

   In lazulite and moonstone—fair to see !

Midway a dais mounted to a bed

Of pearl and ebony, with soft cloths spread.

XII.

Upon the alcove there, and all around

   Love tales were pictured : some swart lady wooed

A lover still unwilling ; he was bound

   In dark warm arms, refusing : then 'twas viewed

How to her spells he melted : then, again,

How what he scorned he sued for—fond and fain.

XIII.

And those who thus Love's luxuries had won

    Asenath seemed, and Yûsuf. Limb for limb,

Lips, eyes, and brows, the Hebrew boy was done

    Lifelike. The gemmed Egyptian dame with him

Shone Asenath herself, Asenath fair,

With robes ungirt, no fillet in her hair!

XIV.

Into this palace 'twas her mind to bring

    Yûsuf the slave, and lead him, room by room,

Through all their passages of pleasuring

    Till eyes' delight should heart's cold doubts consume.

But first herself she 'tired, and lovelier made

That loveliness, too rich before arrayed!

XV

Her eyebrows' arch with pencilled lines she builded,

    And touched each underlid with jetty dye;

Drew the long lashes separate, and gilded

　　Her flesh with palm-flow'r dust, to beautify

The ambered satin of her nape and neck;

And deftly with red henna did she deck

XVI.

Her slender finger-tips; and washed with myrrh

　　Her long black tresses, braiding them in strings

Which, from the queenly gleaming crown of her

　　Swung to her knees, banded with beads and rings:

And, 'thwart her breasts—like lotus-blossoms blown—

A purple, spangled, sindon hath she thrown.

XVII.

Then she bade summon that fair Hebrew boy:

　　Who came, with palms across his faint heart folded,

And kissed her feet, and prayed: "What swift employ

　　May thy true servant find?"　Of manhood moulded

In every part was Yûsuf; and her eye

O'er-roamed him with a tender tyranny.

XVIII.

Yet more he shunned th' imperious look of love

 Than if her glance had blaze of wrath displayed :

" But," quoth the Princess, " this night will I prove

 If thou be servant true ! "   Therewith she bade

Follow :—and, entering that first chamber-door,

Shot the bronze bolt ; and from his brown throat tore —

XIX.

With swift impatient hand—the leathern thong

 Marking him thrall ; and cried : " My soul's desire !

I, thy hid handmaid, do thee daily wrong

 Playing the mistress.   By Ra's morning fire

Freed art thou !   Make my gift of freedom sweet

Lifting this love-sick giver from thy feet ! "

XX.

With that she poured her black imperial hair

 In waves upon his sandals.   But, he said :

"Thou, to whom Egypt's noblest kneel in fear,

    Mock me not thus, on whom the charge is laid

To guard thee for my Lord; or, if set free,

Great lady! grant my soul his liberty!"

XXI.

Silent she rose:—drew him on inwardly

    Behind the second door, locking it hard:

Took from a chest,—cut of the almond-tree—

    A cirque, with gods and scarabs set in sard:

"See now!" she cried: "I crown thee Prince and Lord,

Will not those lips, made royal like mine, afford

XXII.

"The word I pine for, which shall pay for greatness?

    Now may'st thou lift thy face, and answer sweet;

We are as one! Quit shame, forsake sedateness!

    Asenath wooes Lord Yûsuf:—that is meet!"

"Oh, Itfîr's wife!" he said, "meet would it be

I were made vultures' food, hearkening to thee!"

XXIII.

Then, through those chambers third and fourth she passed,

    And to the fifth and sixth she led him on,

Bolting each door behind : till at the last,—

    Laden with gifts of jade, and turkis-stone,

And robes, and torques—she brought Him to her bower,

Where 'twas her thought to put forth Love's last power.

XXIV.

For all four walls with those light pictures burned,

    Painted to life—lovers at play—and these

Asenath seemed, and Yûsuf.   If he turned,

    Unyielding, from the Princess at his knees,

On the same Princess gazed he, imaged sweet ;

And himself yielded, conquered, at her feet.

XXV.

And more than steadfast soul might well withstand

    It was, to bring his troubled gaze again

To that great suppliant, wasting on his hand

   Woeful caressings : and to mark what pain

Filled with clear tears the bright beseeching eyes ;

Heaved the soft breasts, as sea-tides sink and rise.

XXVI.

For, when she linked the last door's chain, and seized

   His hands, and, desperate, her last prayer said,

He had been stone or snow to view, unpleased,

   The lustrous glory of that low-bowed head,

The meekness of such majesty forgot,

The queenly pleading orbs, whose light was shot

XXVII.

Star-wise, through sparkling rain ; which more o'erpowered

   By grace, than greatness, to the sweet surrender.

Like a charmed snake Conscience its cold hood lowered,

   While, soft as muted lute, in accents tender

Her rich lips murmured, " Oh, how long, how long

Wilt thou do thee and me this loveless wrong ? "

XXVIII.

" How long ? when I, who may command, implore,

   Being named Mistress of the Mouths of Nile ?

Yet, if into the Ocean those did pour

   Silver and gold all day, for one kind smile

From those close-curtained eyes, for one light kiss

I would let sea-born Kneph take all of this !

XXIX.

" Give, then, mine heart its will, mine eyelids sleep ;

   My head the pillow that can lull its woe.

Shall Asenath of Memphis vainly weep ?

   I cry to thee by Him thou honourest so,

Thy Hebrew Jah—if He hath any ruth—

Show mercy ! put to fruit thy blossomed youth ! "

XXX.

" Yea ! by the marks thy God hath set on thee

   To make thee most desirable,—thy hair

Glossed like an ibis' wing,—thy brows which be

    Black rainbows to thy sunlike eyes,—the fair

Wonderful rounding of thy temples twain,

And that flower mouth,—which, when it opes again

XXXI.

" Cannot, and shall not say me ' nay '—by these,

    And all thy goodly strength, for Love's use given,

By my salt tears, and by my soul's disease,

    Shut me no longer from the wished-for Heaven ;

Its gate is there ! there—in those arms tight-locked—

Open them—open ! for my heart hath knocked ! "

XXXII.

" What gives thee fear, when I am none afeard ?

    Where is thy shame, if I am naught ashamed ?

What whisper of our comforts shall be heard

    From these still walls ?   How should thy blood be blamed

Mingling with mine, who come of Pharaoh's race ?

With mine, that have these brows, this breast, this face ? "

XXXIII.

" Ah, thou most high and most beguiling one ! "

   Trembling he answered : " tempt me not to this !
Easy it were to do, but ill, being done,

   If I should sell white virtue for a kiss;
And break the bright glass of unstainèd faith
To burn for shame when our Lord Itfîr saith

XXXIV.

" ' Yûsuf, my Trusted ! ' By the living Lord,

   Whose lamp the sun is, seeing everywhere,
Too sore I pity thee ! Too soon the word

   Of ' yea ' would leap, if it were only fear
Which locks it in my lips : oh, let me go
And on some other day this might be so ! "

XXXV

" Nay, nay ! " she cries : " for me is no to-morrow !

   Who, dying in a desert, puts aside

The water-skin?   Who, holding cure of sorrow,
  Bears on with agony?   When could betide
A better time than now, a surer spot?
What's wrought the Gods themselves will witness not!"

XXXVI.

"My God will witness!" quoth he, "and make know
  My Master."   "Oh, thy Master!" brake in she,
"I have a herb of Nile, and, when cups flow,

  Crowned at the banquet, there shall some night be
A strange new savour in his wine:—and, then
Sleep on his eye, and ceasing from 'midst men."

XXXVII.

Backward thereat he drew, as when a snake
  From coralled jaws bares sudden fatal fangs;
But she, distempered, from her belt did take

  A knife: and, while with one fond hand she hangs
Hot on his neck, the other the blade kept
So pressed to the skin the scarlet blood outleapt.

B

XXXVIII.

And with wild eyes she spake: "My soul hath clung
   Too close to thine, Unkind! to cling in vain;
Mine ears have drank the music of thy tongue
   Too long for life, except Love heals life's pain!
See! the fond dagger for my scorned blood yearns,
And drinks its first drop, where the bright point burns!

XXXIX.

"Deny me, and I drive this shining death
   Straight to the heart which thou contemnest so;
And when last love-sigh comes with latest breath,
   And o'er thy cruel hands the red streams flow,
My murdered body shall Lord Itfîr see,
And the dread charge of this will light on thee!"

XL.

With eager grasp he clutched her wrist, and cried:
   "Great Asenath! have pity on us both!

From such mad frenzy turn thy steel aside.

Too fair—too dear—to die! too—" She, not loath,
Deeming the boy relenting, sheathed her blade,
And with close-winding arms a warm chain made

XLI.

About his beating breast, and drew him down

Against her mouth, and dragged " nay! nay!" away
In such a cleaving kiss his sense did swoon,

His tongue, shut in with honey, naught could say;
His eyes, meeting her eyes, such fierce flame took
They dropped their lids not to be lightning-strook.

XLII.

Then, while he sank back, will-less, on the silk,

She rose, of triumph sure, and deftly drew
From her smooth shoulders,—brown and smooth as milk

With palm-wine mixed—that scarf of purple hue
Veiling her bosom's splendours; this she bore,
Quick-tripping, to the niche beside the door,

XLIII.

Where, on tall pedestal, in pride of place,

    Sate Pasht the Cat, with orbs of green and gold;

And, over those green eyes, and o'er the face

    That garment hath she draped, so that its fold

Hid the House-Goddess to her porphyry chin.

" Why doest thou this? " asks Yûsuf.   " If I sin—"

XLIV

Answers glad Asenath—" It must not be

    That Pasht, whom every morn I straitly serve

With musk, and flowers, and prayers—great Pasht, should

        see

    That Pasht, with those sharp eyes, should know I swerve

From law:—for she would blab to Lords of Hell,

But what she doth not spy she will not tell."

XLV.

Turning, she made to clip him; but he broke,

    Like the sun bursting through a shattered cloud,

Fierce from her arms: and, all alight, he spoke

    Angrily thus: "Take, too, thy skirt, and shroud

Yon stars that gaze upon us from God's sky!

Cover, with fine-wove webs, the angry eye

XLVI.

" Of dread Jehovah, watching everywhere!

    Bind His free winds, and bid them whisper naught!

Lay hand upon His lightnings, flashing clear,

    And bribe them not to strike!   Let there be brought

His thunders, muzzled, to thy bower; and win

Their awful voices to forgive our sin!"

XLVII.

" Fear'st thou those stony eyes thou didst enfold,

    And shall not I my fathers' Lord fear more,

Whose glance none may shut out, Whose eyes behold

    All things in every place?   Tempted full sore,

Lady of Egypt! was thy witless slave:

Now breaks he from thee, better faith to save!"

XLVIII.

With that he darted forth.   And Asenath

Reached at his waist-cloth, rending it atwain :

One portion in her wrathful hand she hath,

One the fast-flying Yûsuf doth retain ;

While, in his speed, he flings back bolts and bars

Till, 'scaped, he stands under the mindful stars.

TO A PAIR OF EGYPTIAN SLIPPERS.

Tiny slippers of gold and green,
  Tied with a mouldering golden cord!
What pretty feet they must have been
  When Cæsar Augustus was Egypt's lord!
Somebody graceful and fair you were!
  Not many girls could dance in these!
When did your shoemaker make you, dear,
  Such a nice pair of Egyptian " threes " ?

Where were you measured ?   In Saïs, or On,
  Memphis, or Thebes, or Pelusium ?
Fitting them featly your brown toes upon,
  Lacing them deftly with finger and thumb,
I seem to see you!—so long ago,
  Twenty-one centuries, less or more !

And here are your sandals : yet none of us know
  What name, or fortune, or face you bore.

Your lips would have laughed, with a rosy scorn,
  If the merchant, or slave-girl, had mockingly said,
" The feet will pass, but the shoes they have worn
  Two thousand years onward Time's road shall tread,
And still be footgear as good as new ! "
  To think that calf-skin, gilded and stitched,
Should Rome and the Pharaohs outlive—and you
  Be gone, like a dream, from the world you bewitched !

Not that we mourn you !   'Twere too absurd !
  You have been such a very long while away !
Your dry spiced dust would not value one word
  Of the soft regrets that my verse could say.
Sorrow and Pleasure, and Love and Hate,
  If you ever felt them, have vaporised hence
To this odour—so subtle and delicate—
  Of myrrh, and cassia, and frankincense.

Of course they embalmed you !   Yet not so sweet
 Were aloes and nard, as the youthful glow
Which Amenti stole when the small dark feet
 Wearied of treading our world below.
Look ! it was flood-time in valley of Nile,
 Or a very wet day in the Delta, dear !
When your slippers tripped lightly their latest mile—
 The mud on the soles renders that fact clear.

You knew Cleopatra, no doubt !   You saw
 Antony's galleys from Actium come.
But there ! if questions could answers draw
 From lips so many a long age dumb,
I would not tease you with history,
 Nor vex your heart for the men which were ;
The one point to learn that would fascinate me
 Is, where and what are you to-day, my dear !

You died, believing in Horus and Pasht,
 Isis, Osiris, and priestly lore ;

And found, of course, such theories smashed
    By actual fact on the heavenly shore.
What next did you do?   Did you transmigrate?
    Have we seen you since, all modern and fresh?
Your charming soul—so I calculate—
    Mislaid its mummy, and sought new flesh.

Were you she whom I met at dinner last week,
    With eyes and hair of the Ptolemy black,
Who still of this find in the Fayoum would speak,
    And to Pharaohs and scarabs still carry us back?
A scent of lotus about her hung,
    And she had such a far-away wistful air
As of somebody born when the Earth was young;
    And she wore of gilt slippers a lovely pair.

Perchance you were married?   These might have been
    Part of your *trousseau*—the wedding-shoes;
And you laid them aside with the garments green,
    And painted clay Gods which a bride would use:

And, may be, to-day, by Nile's bright waters
  Damsels of Egypt in gowns of blue—
Great- great- great- — very- great- —grand-daughters
  Owe their shapely insteps to you!

But vainly I beat at the bars of the Past,
  Little green slippers with golden strings!
For all you can tell is that leather will last
  When loves, and delightings, and beautiful things
Have vanished, forgotten—No! not quite that!
  I catch some gleam of the grace you wore
When you finished with Life's daily pit-a-pat,
  And left your shoes at Death's bedroom door.

You were born in the Egypt which did not doubt;
  You were never sad with our new-fashioned
    sorrows:
You were sure, when your play-days on Earth ran
    out,
  Of play-times to come, as we of our morrows!

Oh, wise little Maid of the Delta! I lay

   Your shoes in your mummy-chest back again,

And wish that one game we might merrily play

   At " Hunt the Slipper "—to see it all plain !

THE EGYPTIAN PRINCESS.

THERE was fear and desolation over Egypt's swarthy land
From the holy city of the Sun to hot Syëne's sand:
The sistrum and the cymbal slept, the dancing women
    beat
No measure to the pipe and drum, with silver-slippered
    feet:
For the Daughter of the King must die, the dark
    magicians said
Before once more the Moon-God Khuns should lift his
    hornèd head.

And, all those days, the temple-smoke loaded the heavy
    air
With prayers to Set the Terrible, who heareth not, to
    hear;

Those days the painted flags were down, the festal lamps
 untrimmed,

Mute at their stones the millers ground, silent the Nile
 boats skimmed :

And, through the land, lip passed to lip sad word of what
 would be,

From Nubia's golden mountains to the gateways of the
 Sea.

There, in the Palace Hall, where once her laugh had
 loudest been,

Where, but last Feast Day she had worn the wreath of
 Beauty's Queen,

She lay a lost but lovely thing, the wreath was on her
 brow :

Alas! the lotus could not match its chilly pallor
 now !

And ever as the orb of Day sank lower in the sky,

Her breath came fainter, and the life seemed fading from
 her eye.

Mute o'er the dying maiden's form King Mycerinus
  bends ;—

Not Pharaoh's might from this dread foe proud Egypt's
  hope defends !

Piteously moans he : " In this world, so dark without
  thy smile !

Hast thou one care thy Father's love, thy King's pledge
  may beguile ?

Hast thou a last light wish ?—'Tis thine, by all the Gods
  on high !

If Egypt's blood can win it thee, or Egypt's treasure buy ! "

How eagerly they wait her words ! Upon the pictured
  wall

In long gold lines the dying lights between the columns
  fall ;

Was it strange that tears were glistening where tears
  should never be,

When Death had touched with fatal kiss the lips of such
  as she ?

Was it strange that warriors should raise a very woman's
cry

For help and hope to Athor's ears when such as she must
die ?

Small boot of bearded leeches here ! not all Arabia's
store

Of precious balms can purchase her one noon of sunshine
more !

Hush ! hush ! she speaks !—the pale, drawn lips murmur
a parting speech !

Ah, silence ! let no syllable be lost ! so whispers each.

That grey crow on the Palace wall which croaks and will
not rest,

An archer fits his arrow and splits the evil breast !

"Father ! Great Father !—it is hard,—to die so very
young !

Summer was coming, and I looked to see the palm-buds
sprung !

Must it be always dark like this?—I cannot see thy face!

I am dying! Hold me, Pharaoh! in thy kind and strong
embrace!

List! let them sometimes bear me where the golden sun-
beams lie,

Farewell! Farewell! I know thou wilt! 'Tis easy now
to die!"

And ever when the Star of Kneph has brought the summer
round,

And the Nile rises fast and full along the thirsty ground,

They bear her from her rock-hewn tomb to where the
Sun's broad light

May linger on the close-bound eyes were once so glad and
bright;

And strew palm-clusters on her breast while grey-haired
singers tell

Of the high Egyptian Lady, who loved the Sun so well.

Japanese Poems.

THE GRATEFUL FOXES.

(A Japanese Story, in the Japanese Manner.)

PART I.

In the month when cherry-trees
　　Paint the spring-time pink,
Lady Haru, with her maids,
　　Sate at Kodzu's brink:
Good it is to live on days like these!

Rosy as a Musmee's lips,
　　Red as blood on snow,
Bloomed the jewelled branches forth:
　　Rice-birds chirped below:
Over silver seas went white-sailed ships.

All about the blossoming rape,—
   Glad to own its gold—
Butterflies and dragon-flies
   Flitted ;—snakes were bold
To draw slow coils to sunlight.   Every cape—

From its sleeping shadow rose :
   Fuji-San was seen
Piercing Heaven's blue above,
   Glassed in Ocean's green ;—
Doubled forests, doubled gleaming snows !

Beautiful O Haru San,
   With her maids, at play,
Pulled the lilies ; in the stream
   Bathed, heart-whole and gay :
Spring-time ripples in her sweet veins ran !

By and by, along the river,
   Comes a troop of boys :

'Tis a fox-cub they have captured!
 Laughter loud, and noise
Who shall have its skin, and who its liver.

In the bamboo-thicket's gloom—
 At safe distance—sit
Father fox and mother fox
 Gazing after it :
" O, *Kawwaiso !* Caught when Spring was come ! "

" Cruel, noisy boys ! " she said,
 " Loose the little fox !
See his honourable parents
 Weeping, by the rocks ! "—
" *Iye ! iye !* " Each one shook his head.

" Foxes' skins fetch half a bu
 In Komadzu town !
Foxes' livers—sliced and dried,
 And well powdered down—
Sovereign physic for a fever brew ! "

" Ah ! but when all things rejoice
　　In this flower-time feast : "—
Spake the Princess—" will you kill
　　Such a small, soft beast ? "
" *Hime Sama !* " cried the village boys :

" Your august excuse we crave—
　　Yet—three hundred cash !
When would such a prize befall
　　If, with pity rash,
We this cub unto the old ones gave ? "

Thereupon O Haru San
　　From her girdle drew
Copper money, silver money
　　Till it made a bu.
" See ! take twice the price ! " she said.　　They ran

Merry thence, to be so rich,
　　Leaving frightened, free,

In that lovely lady's lap
  Poor *Ko-Kitsune,*
No more frightened, feeling her soft touch.

For she loosed, with tender hand,
  Knot, and noose, and string :
Stroked the red fur smooth again
  On the ruffled thing ;
Rolled cool *nakasè* to make a band

Round the little bleeding leg :
  Offered fish and rice.
Plain as speech the black eyes said :
  " Oh, that's very nice !
Yet, *go men nasaimashi,* I beg

" Leave, kind Princess ! now to go
  Where my parents wait
Close by yonder bean-straw stacks :
  Sad must be their state :
That is my *Okkâsan,* whining so ! "

Therefore, while the old ones gaze,
  Gently on the ground
Sets she down the wistful cub :
  At one happy bound
Leaps it through the lilies, clears the belt of maize.

Wounded foot forgetting
  To its kind it sped ;
Licked its loving dam all over,
  Licked its father's head :
Gravely those old foxes, left and right,

Looked it over, neck and breast,
  Scanned it up and down,
Smelled it from the feathery brush
  To the smooth brown crown.
Then, upon their haunches humbly dressed,

Two sharp barks of gratitude
  Honourably paid :

"Farewell!   We, your servants three,
  Send you thanks, sweet maid!
Sayonara!"   So they sought the wood.

She, with glad steps, homeward went
  By the river banks,
Watching purple shadows climb
  Fuji's wooded flanks,
Musing how fair Mercy brings Content.

PART II.

IN the tenth Moon—none wist why—
  Sick that Lady lay:
As from cherry boughs the bloom
  Falls, so fell away
Cheeks' fresh tint, and ripe lips' rosy dye.

More and more the gentle face
  Weary grew and wan:
Those that saw her in the Spring-tide—
  Sweet O Haru San—
Cried: "Oh, where is gone such youth and grace?"

Grave physicians gathered nigh
  Famed for healing lore;
Sovereign herbs they culled and boiled :

Not one whit the more
Gained she glow of cheek or light of eye.

"Ever," so she sadly said,
  "In the dead of night,
Something wicked, dreamy, dim
  Seemed to rise in sight,
Hovered—horrible—about her bed."

Therefore, on each side her pillow
  Watched a grey-haired nurse.
In the morning, nothing witnessed!
  Princess Haru worse!
Drooping like a root-cut river-willow.

Six new nurses sate about
  All with lamps alight.
"*Setsunai!*" the Princess cries
  At the dead of night.
All the nurses sleeping, all the lamps gone out!

Thereupon, her maids fourscore
  Kept full watch and ward.
At the " hour of the Rat "
  Each maid sleeping hard!
The torches quenched! the Princess weeping sore!

Next, five councillors of fame,
  Wearing swords and frocks,
Watched, by royal ordinance;
  Yet—at " hour of Ox "
All a-slumber!   Haru plagued the same!

Isahaya Buzen spake:
  " *Maho-tsukai* is here !
'Tis some hellish witchcraft works,
  Else, with one so dear,
All our eyelids heavy what could make ? "

" Is there none to break the spell ?
  Must our Princess die ?

With my fingers and my thumbs
   Held I wide each eye ;
Suddenly, like one a-drunk, I fell ! "

Spake the Chief Priest, Raitan :
   " Nightly, while I pray,
Burning incense-sticks, and beating
   Buddha's drum,—till day,
Standing near the shrine I see a man,

" Handsome, youthful, fixed of face,
   He doth supplicate,
' Set my Lady Haru free
   From her evil state !
Hear the prayer of Itô, Lord of Grace ! '

" ' Tak'st,' I asked him, ' no repose ? '
   ' Holy Sir ! ' he said,
' Prayer is all that I may offer.
   Might I guard her bed
All Hell's fiends these eyes should never close ! '

" Being but your foot-soldier
　Itô dares not speak ! "
Quoth the Shogun, " Let him be
　Taicho—Captain !　Seek
Only how to save our daughter here ! "

Therefore, with those maids fourscore,
　And those statesmen five,
Soldier Itô kept the watch.
　Hardly half-alive
Lay the gentle Lady, moaning sore.

On the snow-white mats a cloth
　Heedfully he spreads ;
Stealthily his dirk he drew ;
　Then—when all their heads
Nodded, at the " hour of the Moth,"

Deep he drives it in his thigh.
　From the smarting wound

Spirts the blood : when slumber tempts
   Twists he that blade round.
Others doze, but Itô shuts no eye !

Soon he sees the Witch appear—
   Oh, a dream of death !
Wolf-shaped ! Wickedly its mouth
   Sucks O Haru's breath.
Itô leaps upon it, free of fear,

Grasps it : flings it : goes to kill !
   Struggling shrieks that Shape :
" If you slay me she must die,
   Grant me hence escape
And I tell what thing might make her well."

" Tell it, Hag !" he cries, " and swear
   Never more to prowl !"
Pants the Witch, " I swear ! If you
   Grate, in her rice-bowl,
Fox's liver, woes will disappear."

Itô from the Night-Wolf tore
  One huge bristling ear.
In the morning all awakened,
  Ah, the joy, the fear!
Haru smiling! Blood upon the floor!

Statesmen five, and waitresses,
  Sore ashamed to drowse!
Gladness in the royal heart,
  Joyaunce in the house!
Itô's hurt O Haru's own hand dresses!

Then he showed the ear, and told them
  How the Witch's breath
Spread a spell of slumber round
  Deep as sleep of death.
" I myself had nodded, but, behold them!

" With these humble wounds to aid
  I remained awake,

Twisting still the dagger slowly :
   Princess ! for thy sake
In my heart I would have turned that blade ! "

Near and far the King's word sped
   Messengers to bring
Fox's liver. " If," quoth he,
   " 'Tis this healing thing
Faithful Itô shall O Haru wed."

PART III.

NEAR and far the hunters sought,
   Roaming every wood:
The court would pay the weight in gold
   'Twas well understood
Yet no fox's liver to be bought!

To their mountain huts again
   Sad those hunters came.
" All the foxes know ! " said they :
   " Far and wide the fame
Passeth of this Princess and her pain."

Wrathful waxed the Lord—spake he
   " Loth I were to slay
One fox even, yet my child

Pines : if not to-day
Comes this thing, then disembowelled be

" Our physicians !   Tell them so !
   Shall a Princess sink
For this matter of one fox ? "
   Sadly sate, to think,
All the great court doctors, in a row.

Then they humbly sent to say :
   " One man might succeed !
Itô—please your Majesty—
   Is the best at need :
Deign to grant for Itô one more day ! "

Itô reached his arrows down,
   Strung his hunting-bow,
Took his knife, and rope, and nets,
   In the woods to go :
Suddenly—at entrance of the town—

Comes a woman, with a jar;

    Very low she bows:

" *Go men nasai !* I was bringing

    This to my Lord's house:

'Tis what you would seek, fetched from afar."

Joyously he prays the price:

    " Nay !" says she,—and drew

Closer down upon her face

    The country hood of blue,—

" Afterwards will very well suffice !"

Joyously he brings it home:

    Glad those doctors grew !

In a bowl of beaten gold

    The precious broth they brew:

The Princess drinks ! the charm is overcome !

Bright as silver star, sprung newly

    From the purple sea,

From her bath she trips, and fastens
   Jiban, imoji,
All the glory of her garments, duly :

In the garden, with her maid,
   Walks, a moving Flower,
Fairer than the Kiku bloom
   After autumn shower.
Quoth the Court, "But, is the bringer paid ? "

" *Tenshi Sama !* " Itô said,
   " Yonder she attends ! "
Quoth he, " Take this gold, and pay
   What may make amends ! "
At the spot they find a dog-fox—dead !

Round its neck cause thus reported :
   " *'Tis my husband here !*
For his child he gives his liver
   To the Princess dear :
I—his very lowly wife—have brought it."

FUJI-YAMA.

To the fairest of his friends
This her faithful poet sends.

  On the top of Fuji-San
Now we stand; and half Japan
Like a mighty map unrolled
Spreads beneath us, green and gold:
Southward, pale and bright, the sea
Shines, from distant Misaki,
Round Atami's broken coast,
Till the silvery gleam is lost,
Mingling with the silvery sky,
Far away toward Narumi:
Northward, yonder line of blue—
Over Mino and Bi-shû—

(Say the guides) is Biwa Lake,

Forty ri removed, to take

The stork's road through the azure air.

Oh, if I had his painted pair

Of wings, I'd fly with them, and lend

Those strong plumes to my gentle friend

That she might come, without one soil

Of dust on her dear feet, or toil

Of weary walking, up this steep

To gaze on the Pacific deep,

Fuji's vast slope—a mountain-world—

With, half-way down, the soft clouds curled

Around her waist, an *obi* fair,

Scarlet and gold, like what you wear.

   The rivers, running far below,

Like white threads on a green cloth show;

The towns are little purple spots,

The villages faint greyish dots;

Over the tallest mountains round

We gaze, from Fuji's monstrous mound,

And see far past them, just as you

Spy Mita clear from Azabu,

O-Yama to a mole-hill shrinks,

Bukôzan, now, one hardly thinks

As high as Kompira, that hill

You climbed, with such good heart and will

At Ikao, in the pelting rain :

We spy those Ikao ranges plain

Beyond Koshiû, and near to view

Karuizawa's green tops, too.

What sunny hours, what lightsome times

We had there, in our walks and climbs !

I like the mountains of Japan

Best, at your side, O Yoshi San !

Gotemba to Subashiri

The road was rough, yet fair to see ;

Red lilies glittered in the grass,

Green waved the rice, as we did pass

Nearer to this majestic Hill,

Which stately grew, and statelier still

In ever-shifting clouded dress

As we drew close; its loveliness

Most perfect when at sunset-time

The mists rolled from its brow sublime

And showed—o'erhanging the long street

(Busy with many a pilgrim's feet

And fluttering with ten thousand flags)—

Proud Fuji to her topmost crags

Steel-blue against a saffron sky—

A Queen! A World! A Mystery!

At daybreak, from Subashiri

We started forth, with horses three,

To thread the woodland path, which leads

By groves and streams and shrines and meads,

Nigher and higher, till we find

Umagaeshi, and leave behind

Our steeds. Henceforward every ri

With sturdy foot must traversed be :
And Fuji, lifting rosy red
Beyond the pines her peerless head,
Seems still as far, as when, last night,
We watched her in the sunset's light.

While yet we paced the forest road
Where green woods made a garment broad
For Fuji's knees, and dappled shade
Upon the speckled pumice played,
I wished you by, that you might share
That sweetness of the upland air
And glow of the glad sunburst, now
Crowning with gold Queen Fuji's brow ;
But when we came where snow-slips tear
The flanks of the red mountain bare,
And thence to climb the cone began,
'Mid dykes and crags, O Yoshi San !
At each hard step I did rejoice
Not to be hearing your soft voice,

And not to see your *zori* tread
That rugged way, which still o'erhead
Zigzagged the shoulder of the crag,
All shifting lava-dust and slag;
Almost for men too steep and rough
Winds the wild path! We had enough
Of breathless, toilsome tramp all day
Before our long line made its way
To "Station Eight"—*Hachi-go-me,*
Glad was I, 'mid such mist and rain
To know you safe in the warm plain.

Clambering from "Station Eight's" black rock
We topped the cone at nine o'clock,
Where this I write, to keep my word,
And prove that, wholly undeterred
By distance, high up in the sky
My thoughts back to my sweet Friend fly
Down from the crest of green Japan
To chat with you, O Yoshi San!

THE MUSMEE.

The Musmee has brown velvet eyes
  Curtained with satin, sleepily;
You wonder if those lids would rise
  The newest, strangest sight to see;
But when she chatters, laughs, or plays
  Kôto, biwa, or samisen,
No jewel gleams with brighter rays
  Than flash from those dark lashes then.

The Musmee has a small brown face,
  " Musk-melon seed " its perfect shape:
Jetty arched eyebrows; nose to grace
  The rosy mouth beneath; a nape,
And neck, and chin, and smooth, soft cheeks
  Carved out of sun-burned ivory,

With teeth, which, when she smiles or speaks,
  Pearl merchants might come leagues to see!

The Musmee's hair could teach the night
  How to grow dark, the raven's wing
How to seem ebon! Grand the sight
  When, in rich masses, towering,
She builds each high black-marble coil,
  And binds the gold and scarlet in;
And thrusts, triumphant, through the toil
  The Kanzâshi, her jewelled pin.

The Musmee has wee faultless feet,
  With snow-white *tabi* trimly decked,
Which patter down the city street,
  In short steps, slow and circumspect;
A velvet string between her toes
  Holds to its place th' unwilling shoe:
Pretty and pigeon-like she goes,
  And on her head a hood of blue.

The Musmee wears a wondrous dress—

Kimono, obi, imoji—

A rose-bush in Spring loveliness

Is not more colour-glad to see!

Her girdle holds her silver pipe,

And heavy swing her long silk sleeves

With cakes, love-letters, *mikan* ripe,

Small change, musk-bag, and writing-leaves.

The Musmee's heart is slow to grief,

And quick to pleasure, dance, and song;

The Musmee's pocket-handkerchief

A square of paper!   All day long

Gentle, and sweet, and debonair

Is, rich or poor, this Asian lass :

Heaven have her in its tender care,

O medetô gozarimas ! *

* Japanese for "May it be well with thee ! "

AN INTRODUCTION.

(To O Yoshi San, with a Copy of "Alice through the
Looking-Glass.")

BLUE-EYED Alice! once more pass

Lightly through your looking-glass,

Where, in wonder-world of dream,

Nothing is, but all things seem.

Pass! and tell O Yoshi San

All the mad wild fun you can,

Till her dear eyes, dark as night,

Gleam like yours with gay delight.

English Alice! if you please,

Be to-day quite Japanese!

Alice! here's O Yoshi San!

(Sweetest maid in all Japan)

Full of fun as heav'n of blue,

Yet demure and studious, too :

Yoshi ! give your soft small hand

To Alice, fresh from Dreaming-Land !

Sweetest girl in England she,

So, make friends—and think of me !

THE EMPEROR'S BREAKFAST.

FIFTEEN centuries ago,
Emperor Nintok of Japan
Walked upon his roof, at morning,
Watching if the work began
Well—to gild the cedar frieze
Of his palace galleries;
Well—to nail the silver plates
Of his inner palace gates;
For the Queen would have it so
Fifteen hundred years ago!

Walking on his roof, he spied
Streets and lanes and quarters teeming
Saw his city spreading wide:
Ah! but poor and sad in seeming

Showed those lowly wooden huts
Underneath the King's gates gleaming.
Oh ! he knows each wicket shuts
One world out and one world in :
This so great, and that so small,
Yet to those plain folks within
The little world their all in all !
Just then, the waiting-maids bore through
The breakfast of King Nintoku.

Quoth the Emperor, gazing round,
" Wherefore—when my meats abound—
See I not more smoke arise
From these huts beneath mine eyes ?
Chimneys jut into the air,
Yet no chimney-reek is there
Telling how the household pot
Bubbles glad with *gohan* * hot !
Gild me no more galleries

* Boiled rice.

If my people lose the gold!
Let my doors unplated go
If the silver leaves them cold!
This city of all tax I ease
For three years : We decree it so!
From those huts there shall be smoke!"
Thus the Emperor Nintok spoke.

Three years sped. Upon his roof
That Monarch paced again. Aloof
His Empress hung, ill-pleased to see
The snows drip through her gallery,
The gates agape for cracks, and grey
With wear and weather. "Consort! say
If thus the Emperor of Japan
Should lodge, like some vile peasant man
Whose thatch leaks for a load of straw?"
"Princess august! what recks a flaw"
Nintok replied, "in gate or wall
When, far and wide, those chimneys all

Fling their blue house-flags to the sky

Where the Gods count them ?   Thou and I

Have part in all the poor folks' health

A people's weal makes a King's wealth !"

"SAYONARA."

WHICH word, of all the words for parting made,

Seems best to say, and sweetest, being said?

Which holds most tenderness, and least despair,

And lingers longest in the loved one's ear?

O Yoshi San! O Fuku San! when we

Must say " Good-bye," shall that the last word be,

Our English " God be with you?" or, in phrase

Of Persia, " *Khuda hafíz*"—" All your days

Heaven keep you!"   Or, as the Egyptians do,

" *Lailatak saïd!*"—" Happy night to you!"

Or, in the Arab manner, hand on brow,

" *Salaam aleikum!*"—" Peace be with you now!"

Or, in the soft Italian—" *Addio!*"

" To God I give you, since—alas!—I go."

" *Ora d' partenza!*"   Or, as they of Spain,

" *Hasta la vista !* "—" Till we meet again ! "

" *Vaya con Dios !* "—" Go thy ways with God ! "

Or lightly, with the lively Frenchman's nod,

" *Bon soir, mais sans adieu !* "—" Good-night, and yet

No speech of parting till once more we are met ! "

Or solemn Sanskrit " *Swâgatam ;* " or word

Of guttural German, at hand-shaking heard,

" *Auf wiedersehen.*" Or any far-fetched speech

Of India, China, Russia, seeking each

Some pretty gentle wish to charm away

The sorrow of the thing they have to say ?

No ! it shall not be any one of these,

But " *Sayonara,*" in soft Japanese ;

For this at worst, means " Since it must be so ! "

And, while we speak the sad word, who can know

We shall not change it to " *So de wa nai !* "

And have no *Sayonara* then to say ?

AT SEA.

TANGLED and torn, the white sea-laces
   Broider the breast of the Indian Deep :
Lifted aloft the strong screw races
   To slacken and strain in the waves which leap :
The great sails swell : the broad bows shiver
   To green and silver the purple sea ;
And, down from the sunset, a dancing river
   Flows, broken gold, where our ship goes free.

Too free ! too fast ! With memories laden
   I gaze to the northward where lies Japan :
Oh, fair and pleasant, and soft-voiced maiden !
   You are there, too distant ! O Yoshi San !
You are under those clouds by the storm-winds shaken,
   A thousand ri, as the sea-gull flies,

As lost as if Death, not Time, had taken
　My eyes away from your beautiful eyes.

Yet, if it were Death, of Friends, my Fairest!
　He could not rend our spirits in twain:
They came too near to be less than nearest
　In the world where true hearts mingle again.
But sad is the hour we sigh farewell in,
　And, for me, whenever they name Japan,
All grace, all charm, of the land you dwell in
　Is spoken in saying "O Yoshi San!"

THE "NO" DANCE.

YAMADA SAN said: "Come, and see the 'No'—
Those songs and dances of our old Japan :—
They make the ancient music faithfully
This evening at my Lord the Governor's ;
You shall be honourably pleased.   What best
Kyoto boasts of geishas will be there,
With Nara's koto-player ; Haru San
To beat the drum.   O Yuki San's the Boy ;
O Tsuru plays the Fairy in first dance —
The 'Feather Dress.'"

                        So to the Governor's
That evening, through the lanes of lamps, we went.

And, when the feast was ended on the mats—
Three sides of a full square of friendliness,

Missing Page

Missing Page

And, behold !

Suddenly—hanging on a branch of fir—
A wondrous sight he spies !   The samisens
Twangle surprise, the drums beat *Hé-hé-hé*,
While Yuki San, a-tiptoe, reaches down
A many-tinctured, fairy-patterned robe—
All gold and scarlet and celestial white—
Of feathers wove, but feathers of such birds
As surely never perched on earthly tree !
The lining shot with airy tender tints
As of a broken rainbow.   Glad he scans
The strange bright treasure-trove.   Another such
Suruga never saw !—Narumi's looms
Never dreamed such a marvel !   Light of heart
Into his hut dances Hakuriyô,
Casting the nets aside to clasp the robe.

Next,—very softly trill the samisens,
The drums beat muted, and the flute pipes forth
Expectant tones, while—light as falling snow

Or breath of morning breeze, whispering its way
Through the awakening maple-leaves—glides in
A Heavenly Fairy! 'Tis O Tsuru San:
And neck, breast, slender little amber limbs
Are bare as the brown sea - sand : just one
    cloth
Tied with a sky-blue string about the waist
Half covers her.   Sweetly and movingly
At the hut-door she sings: "Oh, thou within
That hast my robe of feathers!   Open now
And give what is not thine, but only mine!"

  Then see we (kneeling watchful on the mats)
O Yuki San come tripping from the hut
Clasping the feather dress.   But when she marks
O Tsuru San bowing before the door
Look how she stands—Yuki the Fisher-lad—
Out of his wits with well-shown wonderment!
So beautiful the dark-eyed weeper is
Unclad, and pleading with those lovely tears.

Down on his face falls young Hakuriyô
And thus they talk, with samisens to help:

SHE. "Fisher-boy! give back to me
        The dress I hanged upon the tree!"

HE. "Oh thou! well-clad in beauty bright!
        Form of glory, face of light!
        Honourably deign to tell
        Where such charms celestial dwell.
        What thy name, august, may be,
        Fairest! first reveal to me!"

SHE.   "I am come from Heaven's domain:
        If I spoke it ne'er so plain
        You my name could never hear
        As the Angels say it there.
        Flying past your little star,
        All so fair it looked, afar—
        Silvery sea and snow-tipped hill—

That I had an idle will
Once to set my foolish feet
On those flowers that shone so sweet.
So I laid my robe aside
In the tree which you espied :
And, without it—shame and woe !
To my home I cannot go !"

HE. " Loveliest Lady ! little mind
Had I, at the first, my find
Ever to surrender.   Now
When you deign to tell me how,
If I keep it, you must stay,
No more for your garment pray !"

SHE. " Ah ! why did I quit my sky
Where yon happy sea-birds fly,
And the wild swan spreads her wings
While the wind between them sings ;
And the free storks urge their flight

F

Strong across the spangled night ?

Render back my robe, and soon

I shall soar beyond the Moon,

Thread the star-paths, and pursue

Light and life beyond the blue.

Mortal ! 'tis impiety

Not to give mine own to me ! "

HE. " Always I would have you here,

Fairy ! bright, and sweet, and dear.

Will you not, for love of love

Let go longing for above ?

I would let go all but life

If I might but make you wife ! "

SHE. " Fisher-boy ! this sea of thine

Maddens thee with mighty wine !

Fair thou art : yet thou and I

Are as is the sea and sky,

Which may meet but cannot marry ;

If, for love of you, I'd tarry,
'Twere as though a cloud should wed
With some hill-top.   Soft night sped
Lone the hill rises.   Touch my hand
And better shalt thou understand."

HE.   " I cannot take it !   Plain I see
The soft, smooth skin, so velvety,
Of hand and wrist !   Yet, when I clasp,
It is a mist melts in my grasp.
Now, I would give you back this dress
If you will change such loveliness
To solid flesh, not floating air,
Oh, thou than living flesh more fair ! "

SHE.   " Peace ! most foolish boy and fond !
I am what those are beyond ;
More substantial, didst thou know,
Than this flesh and blood below,
Give me back the robe whereby

I may once more reach my sky,

And, for deed of **gentilesse,**

When I don again my dress,

I will dance, to do thee **pleasure,**

One round of our heavenly measure;

I will sing, to comfort thee,

One strain of the melody

Heard by souls divine, in sphere

Where the Light is lovelier!"

HE. "Ah! to see you fly I dread

When I **yield** this wonder!   Tread

First your measure, **Lady sweet!**

Then I **place** it at your feet."

SHE. "Shame upon thee!   I have heard

Men will break a plighted word,

.   But with us this is not so!

All unveiled the Spirits go;

And **nay is nay,** and **yes is yes:**

I dance not else!   **Give me the dress!**"

Then see we Hakuriyô, blushing deep,

Lay at her foot the golden-feathered gown

Alight with silvery white and scarlet fires.

And while the samisens make chords of joy

O Tsuru kneels, and gathers wistfully

The shining marvel round her shoulders : laughs

For pleasure to be safe re-plumed : then glides—

With voice of melting notes, and paces fair

Falling as light as fir-cones, to the dance :

SHE. " Now it is mine again

   I am fain, I am fain

  To pay you true, as a Spirit should do

   With secrets of Heaven made plain.

  Yet, not for long can I sing this song,

   Nor dance the dance of the skies :

    Your earth shows fair,

    But dense is the air,

  And we wonder not if your eyes

   A very small part of the splendour see

Laid upon river and lea :

Only one gleam of the glory shed

From Fuji's diademed head

Down to this leaf of the momiji-tree

Which knows and courtesys to me :

For I and the maple-leaf are one

 As we hear, as we hear

The tender unnoticed tone

 Of your Earth's voice, ceaseless and clear :

And we move to the swing

Of your star, in the ring

She weaves round the flying Sun ;

 Weaves so—so—so :—

Which the waves understand

And the wind and the sand :

 But you cannot ever know !"

'Twere good you should have watched O Tsuru San

Deftly pace this, with little lifted feet

Shod in the white silk *tabi :* and soft lips

Making the melodies to guide her feet,
The music sitting silent; or, at most,
Dropping a high note in now and again.
Then, with her fan before her face, or waved
In dreamy curves, she sang a verse of Love
We,—and the Fisher-boy—still on our knees.

SHE. " And Love—sweet Love !
   Oh less than the splendour spread
   From Fuji's head
  To the sea, and the grass, and the grove
  Know ye the deep things of this !
  A little men taste its bliss
   In the belov'd one's charms,
   And the close-wound arms,
  And the spirits which almost kiss
Through their dividing bodies ; and delight
Of mother-love and father-love, and friends
Hand-fast, and heart-fast !   But Death's sudden night
Comes ; and in gloom, it seems, Love's sunshine ends.

Thus Love's warm golden wing

    Shields not from shuddering

The souls it covers, chilled with dread to part.

    Ah! could I tell,

    Who see it near and well,

The far truth freely to each beating heart

    Not on your tearful planet once again

    Should Love be pain,

Nor from your blinded eyes should salt tears start.

    But that which I would teach

    Hath in your human speech

No words to name such comfort rich and great ;

    Therefore dream on, asleep,

    And, dreaming, weep !

And wait ! a little,—yet a little wait !"

So, or in suchwise, in soft Japanese,

The ancient *uta* flowed ; and fluttered to it

O Tsuru San's light silks, kirtle and sleeve ;

And closed and opened to it her brown arms ;

While crystal tears stood in her eyes at times
Singing of sorrowful Love.   Till, with a laugh
She stayed, and brake into the Planet Dance:
Joyously circling, singing, beating time :

SHE. " Steps of my silvery star
   Dancing alone, afar
   So still, so slow
   No mortal may know
  How stately her footsteps are ;
Nor what fair music is guide of her feet,
   Solemn and high and sweet ;
   All in a tune
   To the Sun and the Moon,
And the drums that the glad worlds beat.
As long a path as your little orb goes,
From the first of her flowers to the last of her snows
 My white Home sweeps in a night;
 Knowing not haste, knowing no rest,
   For delight

In the life of her silver light

And joy of the wide blue waste,

    Where the Angels pass

    Like fish through the sea's green glass,

But you cannot see that sight!"

And, while we did not speak for wistfulness,

Watching the woven paces, wondering

To note how foot and tongue kept faultless time

To dreamy tinkling of the samisens,

Across her breast that golden-feathered gown

Softly she drew; spread her brown arms like wings

And passed!—O Yuki San and we alone!

The "No" Dance ended!

                        "Thanks, dear Tsuru San!

Yet half we wish O Yuki had not given!"

Other Poems.

A SONG.

ONCE—and only once—you gave
   One rich gift, which Memory
Shuts within itself, to save
   Sweet and fresh, while life may be :
Shuts it like a rose-leaf treasured
   In the pages of a book,
Which we open, when heart-leisured,
   Now and then—softly to look.

If I told you of that gift
   How and when, the tend'ring of it,
Would you, out of rose-leaf thrift,
   Claim from me the rend'ring of it ?

That might make it two for one
　　('Twas of such unwonted kind!)
Half a mind I have to tell you
　　Not to tell you half a mind.

MOTHERS.

(A Dialogue at Boston, Mass., U.S.A.)

" SEE there," he said, " my fair American !
    Yon noisy child
I'd like to choke, being but ' brutal man ; '
    That Mother mild

" Takes all its howls for music, comforts it
    With song and kiss :
And gives it, at the loudest of its fit,
    Her milky bliss.

" And there again,—yon little lambkin bleating,
    Made for mint-sauce :
At its first cry the Ewe quits clover-eating
    And runs, perforce.

" And yet again, that purple-winged hen-starling,
　　　Hungry—I'll vouch it !
Flies with a fat grub to her nested darling,
　　　Nor dreams to pouch it !

" She-mercy everywhere, she-pitying
　　　In helpless season !
You Boston girls seem up to everything :
　　　Tell me the reason."

" Why, certainly !" she smiled, " don't poets know
　　　Better than others ?
God can't be always everywhere : and, so,
　　　Invented Mothers."

INSCRIPTION FOR STAINED-GLASS
WINDOW

IN ST. MARGARET'S CHURCH, WESTMINSTER, LONDON.

(To the Memory of Edward Lloyd, Esq.)

A MASTER-PRINTER of the Press, he spake
  By mouth of many thousand tongues: he swayed
The pens which break the sceptres.   Good Lord! make
  Thy strong ones faithful and thy bold afraid!

SONNET TO AMERICA

AMERICA! At this thy Golden Gate,

  New travelled from those portals of the West,

  Parting—I make my reverence! It were best

With backward looks to quit a Queen in state!

Land of all lands most fair, and free, and great,

  Of countless kindred lips, wherefrom I heard

Sweet speech of Shakespeare—keep it consecrate

  For noble uses! Land of Freedom's Bird,

  Fearless and proud! so let him soar that, stirred

By generous joy, all lands may learn from thee

  A larger life, and Europe, undeterred

By ancient dreads, dare also to be free

Body and Soul, seeing thine eagle gaze

Undazzled, upon Freedom's sun full-blaze.

THE BRITISH EMPIRE.

FROM CLAUDIAN.

(De secundo Consulatu Stilichonis.)

" Hæc est in gremium Victos quoe sola recepit
  Humanumque genus communi nomine fovit
  Matris non dominœ ritu : civesque vocavit
  Quos domuit, nexuque pio longinqua revinxit."

SHE alone knew, of victors first and best,
To fold the vanquished to her pardoning breast :
To gather 'neath her wings, in one great brood,
The tribes of Man, by might, then love, subdued,
Mother, not Queen, calling those sons by birth
Whom she had conquered—linking ends of Earth.

THE SULTAN'S RING.

(From the Persian.)

A NECK-EXALTING Lord, a Median King,
Heard one in rags, sore-troubled, say this thing
Under the palace-arch—haggard and faint
Rocking upon the Carpet of Complaint:
"Oh, Sultan! to the Door of God goest thou
As I to thine: therefore accomplish now
Mercy towards me, as thou for mercy prayest :
'Make glad my heart!' To Allah so thou sayest,
Therefore, from Sorrow's darkness bring forth mine!"
Now, on that Sultan's thumb a stone did shine,
Pigeon-blood ruby, such a gem the Shroff
Faltered in telling what would weigh enough
In gold tomâns to price it. In the night
It glowed as Day had dropped spark of rose-light

From th' afternoon : and in the Day it seemed
As though a red imprisoned sunbeam gleamed.

The Sultan drew this wonder from his thumb,
While, at his stirrup-iron, grim and dumb,
The Aghas watched, stroking their beards.   He drew
The ruby off, and quotha : " It was new
Upon our lips that prayer !   God may delay
To hear us if we turn our hearts away
When others ask.   Go, sell this ring, and buy
Oil of Content for Sore of Misery ! "

Better a king's hand lacking royal seal
Than king's ear guilty of unheard appeal !

CHAPTER I. OF THE DHAMMAPADA.

THOUGHT in the mind hath made us. What thou art
  By thought was wrought and builded. If a soul
Hath evil thoughts, pain comes as wheels of cart
  Behind its oxen roll.

All that we are is what we think and will:
  Our thoughts shape us and frame. If one endure
In purity of thought, joy follows still
  As his own shadow—sure!

" He hath defamed me, wronged me, broken trust,
  Abased me, beaten me!" If one shall keep
Thoughts like these angry words within his breast
  Hatreds will never sleep!

" He hath defamed me, wronged me, vilely wrought,
   Abased me, beaten me ! "   If one shall send
Such angry words away for pardoning thought
   Hatreds will have an end.

For, never anywhere at any time
   Did hatred cease by hatred.   Always 'tis
By Love that hatred ceaseth.   From the prime
   The ancient Rule is this.

The many, who live foolish, do forget
   Or never knew, how mortal wrongs pass by :
But they who know, and who remember, let
   Transient quarrels die.

Whoso abides, looking for pleasures, vain,
   Gluttonous, proud, in idle luxuries,
Mâra will him o'erthrow, as wind and rain
   Level short-rooted trees.

Whoso abides, disowning joys, controlled,
　　Temperate, faithful, firm, shunning all ill,
Mâra shall no more shake that man strong-souled
　　Than the wind doth a hill.

Whoso *Kâshya* bears—the yellow dress—
　　Being *anishkashya*,* not sin-free
Nor heeding Truth and Law—in wrongfulness
　　That holy robe wears he.

But whoso, living *nishkashya* aright,
　　Clean from offence, doth still in virtue dwell
Observing temperance and truth—that wight
　　Weareth *Kashya* well.

Whoso imagines truth in the untrue
　　And in the true finds untruth—he expires
Never attaining Knowledge—life's to rue
　　He follows vain desires.

---

* There is a play here on the words **Kashya**, the yellow robe of the
Buddhists, and Kashya, "impurity."

Whoso discerns in truth the true, and sees
　　The false in falseness with unblinded eye,
He doth attain to knowledge.　Life with these
　　Aims well before they die.

As rain breaks through an ill-thatched roof, so break
　　Passions through minds which holy thoughts despise :
As rain runs from a well-laid roof—so shake
　　Their passions off, the wise.

The Evil-doer mourneth this life long
　　And mourneth in the life to come.　In both
He grieveth.　When he seeth fruit of wrong
　　To see he will be loath.

The righteous man in this world hath his boot,
　　And in the world to come.　From both he takes
Pleasaunce.　When he doth see his works bear fruit
　　The good sight gladness makes.

Glad is he living, glad in dying, glad
   Having once died: glad alway, glad to know
What good deeds he had done, glad that he had
   More good where he did go.

The lawless man, who Law not following,
   Leaf after leaf recites, and line by line;
No Buddhist is he, but a hireling
   Who counts another's kine.

The law-obeying, loving one who learns
   Only one verse of Dharma, but hath ceased
From envy, hatred, malice, ill concerns,
   He is the Buddhist Priest!

THE CHIPMUNK.

STROLLING in the city garden
Where the gardens touched the woodlands
(Always with new eyes beholding
Men and beasts and birds and flowers
In your land, so fair and friendly,
In America so wondrous);
Suddenly I spy, careering,
Tail in air, alert, observant,
Glittering with black-beady eyeballs
On the rail-edge, like rope-dancer,
Some small beast not known in England.
"What is that?" I said, inquiring,
"Can it be Longfellow's squirrel,
Hiawatha's Adjidaumo?"

" Say ! and don't you really know him ? "
Laughingly replied my comrade,
Tan-faced, prairie boy of ten ;
" That's the Chipmunk, and we kill him
For his smooth, grey, stripey skin."

" Ah ! " I said, " don't kill the Chipmunk,
If his little coat has stripes !
Brother he must be, or cousin
To a chipmunk that I know
Dwelling in the Indian Jungle.
No one kills the small Geloori
Over there in far-off India,
Ever since they heard the story
How its coat came to be striped."

" Why, do tell ! " cried my companion ;
And I told the Hindoo story
All to save chipmunks and squirrels.

Once, among the palm-groves wandering,

Shiva, Lord and God of all things,

By the sea-shore saw a squirrel

Grey, with bushy tail and bright eyes,

Dipping constantly in ocean—

Dipping twenty times a minute,

Dipping deeply in the salt waves

Bushy tail, and then besprinkling

On the shore the gathered water.

Quoth the God, " What art thou doing,

Little grey, insensate Squirrel!

Dipping in the mighty ocean

Tail so insignificant ?"

And the Squirrel meekly answered :

" Oh, Creator of all living,

Glorious Shiva ! I am trying

To bale dry the Indian Sea ;

For there came a furious tempest

Which laid low this lofty palm-tree
Where I built my happy nest;
And the palm has fallen seaward,
And the nest lies in the water,
And my wife and pretty children
In the nest will float away;
Therefore, all the night and day here
Do I dip my tail and shake it,
Hoping, if I labour stoutly,
At the last to bale the sea dry,
So that I may save my darlings
Even though I spoil my tail."

Gravely spake the Lord of Heaven:
" Truly 'tis a good example,
Little, grey, absurd Geloori!
Which you set to families.
If all husbands were as faithful,
And all fathers proved as fond,
Happier would be those I fashion,

Sweet would pass the lives I give!"
Then He stooped, and, with His great hand—
Hand that makes the men and spirits—
Hand that holds the stars and planets
As we grasp a bunch of grapes—
Shiva stroked the toiling squirrel;

And there came, from nose to tail-end,
Four green stripes upon the grey;
Marks by the Supreme Hand planted
As a sign of love forever.
Then He lifted high that hand,
Waved it to the rolling waters,
Waved it to the roaring Main,
Which ran back with all its surges
Like white dogs that know their master,
Leaving bare the rocks and seaweed,
Leaving high and dry the palm-tree.

And the little squirrel hastened—
Cocking high his tail again,

Reached his woven house of grass-blades—
Found his wife, and found his children
Dry and well, and chirping welcomes.
So he brought them safe to dry land,
But the wonder was to see
All their little smooth backs " stripey "
With the sign of Shiva's fingers !

That is why, in distant India,
Good men never kill the chipmunks ;
And, I think, his cousins here,
Though no God has ever stroked them,
Would be grateful if you left them
Playing 'mid the scarlet maples
Of your Pennsylvanian woods.

A ROSE OF THE "GARDEN OF FRAGRANCE."

(From the Persian of Sâdi's "Bostan.")

Of hearts disconsolate see to the state:
To bear a breaking heart may prove thy fate.

Help to be happy those thine aid can bless,
Mindful of thine own day of helplessness.

If thou at others' doors need'st not to pine
In thanks to Allah drive no man from thine.

Over the orphan's path protection spread!
Pluck out his heart-grief, lift his drooping head.

When with his neck bent low thou spiest one,
Kiss not the lifted face of thine own son!

Take heed these go not weeping.   Allah's throne
Shakes to the sigh the orphan breathes alone.

With kindness wipe the tear-drop from his eye,
Cleanse him from dust of his calamity !

There was a merchant, who, upon his way—
Meeting one fatherless and lamed—did stay

To draw the thorn which pricked his foot ; and passed :
And 'twas forgot : and the man died at last :

But in a dream the Prince of Khojand spies
That man again, walking in Paradise ;

Walking and talking in the Blessed Land,
And what he said the Prince could understand :

For he said this : plucking the heavenly posies,
" Ajâb ! that one thorn made me many Roses ! "

TO MY BIOGRAPHER.

TRACE me through my snow,
Track me through my mire,
You shall never know
Half that you desire!

Praise me, or asperse,
Deck me, or deride ;
In my veil of verse
Safe from you I hide.

A PICTURE.

(From the German of the Queen of Roumania.)

Sits upon the splintered summit
Swathed in tempest, by a black gulf,
Wondrous beautiful, a Woman—
Large and strong her body's lines are
As she leans upon the rock
At the crag's edge lightly swaying:
One knee rests across the other
Balanced, and, with fingers clenched,
In her hand she grasps a serpent,
Careless how the monstrous creature
Twines and coils, and shoots its fork forth
Helpless that white grip to loosen,
Helpless to escape her fingers.
Red her hair is; like to flame-tongues

Stream amid the storm its tresses,
Float into the clouds and capture
The chain-lightning as it falls,
Drawing through its skeins those flashes
Which glide harmless down her body,
But, beneath her, split a pine-tree
From its topmost bough to foot.
And the eyes of that wild woman,
In the light which flickers purple
Round and round the summit, glitter
Green beneath great brows of black.

DURCH DEN WALD.

(From the German of the Queen of Roumania.)

THROUGH the forest there fluttered a song
   Upborne upon airy gay wings:
As the breeze lisps the beech-boughs among
   So softly it lit on my strings:
And my harp told the River again:
And the trees and the birds caught the strain:
   And the flow'rs set up soft whisperings.

Through the forest came loitering Love:
   There was budding and blooming at this:
The birds woke, with welcome, the grove
   And the rocks and the springs felt the bliss;
It seemed 'twould be sunshine forever
As the sun shed red gold on the River
   And the waves and the bank-buds did kiss.

Missing Page

THE TOPSAIL OF THE VICTORY.

("On the wall is suspended the foretopsail of Lord Nelson's
flagship Victory." *Vide* "Catalogue of Naval Exhibition, Chelsea,
1891.")

Oh, Wings of Victory!

Proud battle-plumage, torn with shot and ball,

Draped in wide tattered glory on this wall!

Come hither!   Come and see!

Lord Nelson's canvas here!

The topsail of his Flagship, when he sailed

To win Trafalgar for us,—and prevailed

'Mid thunder, flame, and fear.

The cloths she sheeted home

Shining and white that day! hallyard and clew,

Cringle and tack and bolt-rope—clean and new—

Close to the foe to come:

Now faded, ragged, frayed:
As yellow as King George's guineas! Rent
From bunt to ear-ring: yet magnificent!
  Yet in royal state arrayed!

 For, dear and dauntless ship,
Built of the British Oak, and manned with hearts
Staunch as the heart of oak! What pulse but
    starts?
  What pride leaps to the lip

  Thinking how each clout heard
The boatswain pipe: "Hoist the foretopsail, Lads!
Haul home! Haul home!" And then it soars and
    spreads
  Like pinion of sea-bird:

  Amongst the clouds a cloud:
And then it sees from foretop—while it holds
The Spanish breeze, and mightily unfolds—
  Down on the decks that crowd

Of Nelson's lions stand,
Stripped to the waist at stations: every man
Alight with the great signal-words which ran
    Joyous, and good, and grand—

    "*England expects
That every man this day*"—" Ay! ay! we hear!
Our duty we shall do: have ye no fear."
    The very cannons' necks

    Lean hungry o'er the swell,
Craving for battle-food: and, leading all
Nelson's Three-decker goes, majestical!
    Beautiful! terrible!

    Oh, Wings of Victory!
Flew ye indeed that forenoon, white and great,
Wafting our hero to his glorious fate
    Over the dancing sea?

    Marked ye, indeed,
The haughty foemen's challenge-flags unfold

From ship to ship, along the rippled gold?
  And, ever true at need

  Collingwood close?   And Lake?
And Nelson, from his knees, come brave and gay
To give his bright blood for us? and the array
  Of liners, in his wake?

  Gods! How we see
Bullets and round-shot rend thy bellying white!
And scarlet smoke-wreaths from the rattling fight
  Enwrap thee, weather and lee!

  And how, below,
'Mid blast of such red thunders, rife with death,
Such terror as no tempest witnesseth,
  Our British Jacks, aglow

  Fight on for Britain's Crown
As if each man were not King's man, but King!
And what cheers split the sky, when fluttering,
  Flag after flag comes down!

And then—there! there!
While thy scorched folds flap triumph—that 'curst ball!
The mortal wound! our matchless Champion's fall!
  Loss that made all gain dear.

  Foretopsail old!
Under your foot he fell—splendid in death:
Under your shade breathed forth his patriot breath!
  Ah! wove with valour's gold.

  Heroic Rags!
Flaunt to the world, as once to France and Spain,
Token of England's might upon the main,
  Better than blazoned flags.

  Flaunt!—for ye may—
Tatters which make it boast enough to be
Of Nelson's blood! Torn Wings of Victory
  From dread Trafalgar's day!

THE FRIGATE ENDYMION.

("Towards the close of the war with France, Captain the Hon. Sir Charles Paget, while cruising in the Endymion frigate on the coast of Spain, descried a French ship of the line in imminent danger, embayed among rocks on a lee shore : bowsprit and foremast gone, and riding by a stream cable, her only remaining one.

"Though it was blowing a gale, Sir Charles bore down to the assistance of his enemy, dropped his sheet-anchor on the Frenchman's bow, buoyed the cable, and veered it across his hawser. This the disabled ship succeeded in getting in, and thus seven hundred lives were saved from destruction.

"After performing this chivalrous action the Endymion, being herself in great peril, hauled to the wind, let go her bower-anchor, club-hauled, and stood off shore on the other tack." *Vide* "Catalogue Royal Naval Exhibition, 1891.")

THE English roses on her face

   Blossomed a brighter pink, for pride,

As, through the glories of the place

   Wistful, we wandered, side by side.

We saw our bygone worthies stand,
   Done to the life, in steel and gold,
Howard and Drake—a stately band—
   Sir Walter, Anson, Hawkins bold :

By all the martial blazonry
   Of Blake's great battles, and the roar
Of Jervis, thundering through the sea
   With Rodney, Hood, and fifty more :

To him, the bravest, gentlest, best,
   Duty's dear Hero, Britain's star—
The chieftain of the dauntless breast,
   Nelson, our Thunderbolt of War !

We saw him gathering sword by sword
   On conquered decks from Don and Dane,
We saw him Victory's laurelled Lord
   Rend the French battle-line a-twain :

We saw the coat, the vest he wore
   In thick of dread Trafalgar's day :
The blood-stains, and the ball which tore
   Shoulder-gold, lace, and life away.

In countless grand War-pieces there
   The green seas foamed with gallant blood :
The skies blazed high with flame and fear,
   The tall masts toppled to the flood.

But ever, 'mid red rage and glow
   Of each tremendous Ocean fight,
Safe, by the strength of those below
   The flag of England floated bright !

" Ah, dear, brave souls ! " she said, " 'tis good
   To be a British girl and claim
Some drops, too, of such splendid blood,
   Some distant share of deathless fame ! "

" Yet, still I think of what tears rained
　　From tender French and Spanish eyes
For all those glorious days we gained.
　　Oh ! the hard price of victories ! "

" Come then ! " I said : " witness one fight
　　With triumph crowned, which cost no tear :
Waged gallant 'gainst the tempest's might."
　　Then turned we to a canvas near.

" Look ! the King's frigate : and her foe :
　　The coast is Spain !   Cruising to spy
An enemy, she finds him so,
　　Caught in a death-trap, piteously ! "

" A great Three-decker !   Close a-lee
　　Wild breakers on the black rocks foam
Will drown the ship's whole company
　　When that one Anchor's fluke comes home.

" Her foremast gone, she cannot set
   Head-sails to cast her off the land :
Those poor souls have to draw breath, yet
   As long as while a warp will stand.

" 'Tis war-time—time of mutual hate—
   Only to keep off, therefore,—tack,
Mark from afar ' Jean Crapaud's ' fate,
   And lightly to ' my Lords ' bear back

" Good news of the great Liner, done
   To splinters, and some thirty score
Of ' Mounseers ' perished ! Not a gun
   To fire ! Just stand by—no more !

" Also, that Captain who should go—
   Eyes open—where this Gaul is driven,
Would steer straight into Hell's mid woe
   Out of the easy peace of Heaven.

I

" Well! let them strike and drown!   Not he!
   Not lion-hearted Paget!   No!
The war's forgot!   He'll make us see
   Seamanship at its topmost.   Blow

" Boatswain! your pipe!   Endymions, hear!
   Forward and aft, all hands on deck!
Let my sails draw, range hawsers clear!
   Paget from Fate his foe will pluck!"

" So bears she down : the fair white flag
   Hoisted—full friendly—at the main!
Her guns run in : twice to a rag
   The stormsail torn : but set again.

" And when she rounds to wind, they swarm
   Into their rigging, and they dip
The tricolor, with hearts made warm
   By hope and love.   Look now! his ship

"Inside the doomed one! and you note
　　How, between life and death, he keeps
His Frigate like a pleasure-boat
　　Clean full and by: and, while he sweeps

" Athwart the Frenchman's hawse, lets go
　　His big sheet-anchor: buoys it, cast
Clear o'er the rail.　They know, they know!
　　Here's help! here's hope! here's chance at last!

" For hauling (you shall understand)
　　The English hawser o'er her side,
All fear is fled of yon black strand:
　　Safely the huge Three-decker rides.

" Safe shall she come to Brest again,
　　With Jean and Jacques, and Paul and Pierre;
And float to fight King George's men
　　Thanks to the goodly British gear.

" But woe to bold Endymion,
　　Never was darker plight for craft ;
Laid-to—all save one anchor gone,
　　And those black fateful rocks abaft !

" Fresh-plucked from death the Frenchmen watched
　　A sailor's highest lesson shown ;
They view by skill that Frigate snatched
　　From peril direr than their own.

" To beat to windward she must fly
　　Round to the starboard tack : but drives
Full on the rocks in staying : try
　　To wear her, the same fate arrives.

" One desperate shift remains !　She brings
　　Her cable to the bitts : makes fast ;
Drops anchor : by the starboard swings :
　　And, when a-lee her stern is cast,

" Hauls on the slack, and cuts adrift :
   Sheets home her foresail : fills, and swerves
A ship's length forth. Subtle and swift
   Her aim the tempest's wrath now serves.

" In view of those safe, rescued men,
   Foot by foot steals she space to live :
Self-stripped of hope, except she win
   The offing. None can succour give !

" A ship's length more ! One ship's length more !
   And then ' helm down ! ' Then, something free
Comes the fierce blast ! That leeward shore
   Slides slow astern ! That raging sea

' Widens ! If once yon whitened reef
   She weathers ! 'tis a saviour saved !—
Seamanship conquers ! Past belief
   She rounds ! The peril hath been braved !

"Then, louder than the storm-wind's yell,

    Rings in her wake the Frenchmen's cheer,

Bidding the good ship glad farewell

    While our staunch Frigate draws out clear.

" Never was nobler salvage made !

    Never a smarter sea-deed done ! "

" Best of all fights I love," she said :

    " This fight of the Endymion."

L'ENVOI.

(From the German of the Queen of Roumania.)

AND that which here I have been singing
   It was all yours—not mine !
From your joy all its gladness bringing :
Its sad chords from your sorrows ringing :
   I did but you divine !

Yours were the thoughts forever ranging !
   You made the folk-tales true !
In this Earth-show of chance and changing,
Of life uniting, death estranging,
   Look, Soul ! these things were you !

Perchance when Death shall give me leisure,
  And these tired lips lie dumb,
Then you my words will better measure,
And in my love take larger pleasure,
  Its meaning being come!

THE END.

PRINTED BY BALLANTYNE, HANSON AND CO.
EDINBURGH AND LONDON.

A CATALOGUE OF WORKS

IN

GENERAL LITERATURE

PUBLISHED BY

MESSRS. LONGMANS, GREEN, & CO.,

89 PATERNOSTER ROW, LONDON, E.C.

MESSRS. LONGMANS, GREEN, & CO.

Issue the undermentioned Lists of their Publications, which may be had post free on application :—

1. MONTHLY LIST OF NEW WORKS AND NEW EDITIONS.
2. QUARTERLY LIST OF ANNOUNCEMENTS AND NEW WORKS.
3. NOTES ON BOOKS; BEING AN ANALYSIS OF THE WORKS PUBLISHED DURING EACH QUARTER.
4. CATALOGUE OF SCIENTIFIC WORKS.
5. CATALOGUE OF MEDICAL AND SURGICAL WORKS.

6. CATALOGUE OF SCHOOL BOOKS AND EDUCATIONAL WORKS.
7. CATALOGUE OF BOOKS FOR ELEMENTARY SCHOOLS AND PUPIL TEACHERS.
8. CATALOGUE OF THEOLOGICAL WORKS BY DIVINES AND MEMBERS OF THE CHURCH OF ENGLAND.
9. CATALOGUE OF WORKS IN GENERAL LITERATURE.

ABBEY (Rev. C. J.) and OVERTON (Rev. J. H.).—THE ENGLISH CHURCH IN THE EIGHTEENTH CENTURY. Cr. 8vo. 7s. 6d.

ABBOTT (Evelyn).—A HISTORY OF GREECE. In Two Parts.
Part I.—From the Earliest Times to the Ionian Revolt. Cr. 8vo. 10s. 6d.
Part II. Vol. I.—500-445 B.C. [*In the Press.*] Vol. II.—[*In Preparation.*]

———— HELLENICA. A Collection of Essays on Greek Poetry, Philosophy, History, and Religion. Edited by EVELYN ABBOTT. 8vo. 16s.

ACLAND (A. H. Dyke) and RANSOME (Cyril).—A HANDBOOK IN OUTLINE OF THE POLITICAL HISTORY OF ENGLAND TO 1890. Chronologically Arranged. Crown 8vo. 6s.

ACTON (Eliza).—MODERN COOKERY. With 150 Woodcuts. Fcp. 8vo. 4s. 6d.

A. K. H. B.—THE ESSAYS AND CONTRIBUTIONS OF. Crown 8vo. 3*s*. 6*d*. each.

Autumn Holidays of a Country Parson.	**Leisure Hours in Town.**
Changed Aspects of Unchanged Truths.	**Lessons of Middle Age.**
	Our Little Life. Two Series.
Commonplace Philosopher.	**Our Homely Comedy and Tragedy.**
Counsel and Comfort from a City Pulpit.	**Present Day Thoughts.**
	Recreations of a Country Parson.
Critical Essays of a Country Parson.	Three Series.
East Coast Days and Memories.	**Seaside Musings.**
Graver Thoughts of a Country Parson.	**Sunday Afternoons in the Parish Church of a Scottish University City.**
Three Series.	
Landscapes, Churches, and Moralities.	

———— 'To Meet the Day' through the Christian Year ; being a Text of Scripture, with an Original Meditation and a Short Selection in Verse for Every Day. Crown 8vo. 4*s*. 6*d*.

AMERICAN WHIST, Illustrated : containing the Laws and Principles of the Game, the Analysis of the New Play. By G. W. P. Fcp. 8vo. 6*s*. 6*d*.

AMOS (Sheldon).—A PRIMER OF THE ENGLISH CONSTITUTION AND GOVERNMENT. Crown 8vo. 6*s*.

ANNUAL REGISTER (The). A Review of Public Events at Home and Abroad, for the year 1890. 8vo. 18*s*.
   . Volumes of the 'Annual Register' for the years 1863-1889 can still be had.

ANSTEY (F.).—THE BLACK POODLE, and other Stories. Crown 8vo. 2*s*. boards. ; 2*s*. 6*d*. cloth.

———— VOCES POPULI. Reprinted from *Punch*. First Series, with 20 Illustrations by J. BERNARD PARTRIDGE. Fcp. 4to. 5*s*.

ARISTOTLE—The Works of.

———— THE POLITICS, G. Bekker's Greek Text of Books I. III. IV. (VII.), with an English Translation by W. E. BOLLAND, and short Introductory Essays by ANDREW LANG. Crown 8vo. 7*s*. 6*d*.

———— THE POLITICS, Introductory Essays. By ANDREW LANG. (From Bolland and Lang's 'Politics'.) Crown 8vo. 2*s*. 6*d*.

———— THE ETHICS, Greek Text, illustrated with Essays and Notes. By Sir ALEXANDER GRANT, Bart. 2 vols. 8vo. 32*s*.

———— THE NICOMACHEAN ETHICS, newly translated into English. By ROBERT WILLIAMS. Crown 8vo. 7*s*. 6*d*.

ARMSTRONG (Ed.).—ELISABETH FARNESE : the Termagant of Spain.

ARMSTRONG (G. F. Savage-).—POEMS : Lyrical and Dramatic. Fcp. 8vo. 6*s*.

BY THE SAME AUTHOR. Fcp. 8vo.

King Saul. 5*s*.	**Stories of Wicklow.** Poems. 9*s*.
King David. 5*s*.	**Mephistopheles in Broadcloth ; a Satire.** 4*s*.
King Solomon. 6*s*.	
Ugone ; a Tragedy. 6*s*.	**The Life and Letters of Edmond J. Armstrong.** 7*s*. 6*d*.
A Garland from Greece. Poems. 9*s*.	

ARMSTRONG (E. J.).—POETICAL WORKS. Fcp. 8vo. 5*s*.
———— ESSAYS AND SKETCHES. Fcp. 8vo. 5*s*.

ARNOLD (Sir Edwin).—THE LIGHT OF THE WORLD, or the Great Consummation. A Poem. Crown 8vo. 7s. 6d. *net.*

———— SEAS AND LANDS. Reprinted by the permission of the proprietors of the *Daily Telegraph*, from Letters published under the title 'By Sea and Land' in that Journal. Illustrated. 8vo. 21s.

ARNOLD (Dr. T.).—INTRODUCTORY LECTURES ON MODERN HISTORY. 8vo. 7s. 6d.

———— MISCELLANEOUS WORKS. 8vo. 7s. 6d.

ASHLEY (J. W.).—ENGLISH ECONOMIC HISTORY AND THEORY. Part I.—The Middle Ages. Crown 8vo. 5s.

ATELIER (The) du Lys; or, An Art Student in the Reign of Terror. By the Author of 'Mademoiselle Mori'. Crown 8vo. 2s. 6d.

BY THE SAME AUTHOR. Crown 2s. 6d. each.

MADEMOISELLE MORI.	A CHILD OF THE REVOLU-
THAT CHILD.	TION.
UNDER A CLOUD.	HESTER'S VENTURE.
THE FIDDLER OF LUGAU.	IN THE OLDEN TIME.

BACON.—COMPLETE WORKS. Edited by R. L. ELLIS, J. SPEDDING, and D. D. HEATH. 7 vols. 8vo. £3 13s. 6d.

———— LETTERS AND LIFE, INCLUDING ALL HIS OCCASIONAL WORKS. Edited by J. SPEDDING. 7 vols. 8vo. £4 4s.

———— THE ESSAYS; with Annotations. By Archbishop WHATELY. 8vo. 10s. 6d.

———— THE ESSAYS; with Introduction, Notes, and Index. By E. A. ABBOTT. 2 vols. Fcp. 8vo. 6s. Text and Index only. Fcp. 8vo. 2s. 6d.

BADMINTON LIBRARY (The), edited by the DUKE OF BEAUFORT, assisted by ALFRED E. T. WATSON.

HUNTING. By the DUKE OF BEAUFORT, and MOWBRAY MORRIS. With 53 Illustrations. Crown 8vo. 10s. 6d.

FISHING. By H. CHOLMONDELEY-PENNELL.
Vol. I. Salmon, Trout, and Grayling. 158 Illustrations. Crown 8vo. 10s. 6d.
Vol. II. Pike and other Coarse Fish. 132 Illustrations. Crown 8vo. 10s. 6d.

RACING AND STEEPLECHASING. By the EARL OF SUFFOLK AND BERKSHIRE, W. G. CRAVEN, &c. 56 Illustrations. Crown 8vo. 10s. 6d.

SHOOTING. By LORD WALSINGHAM, and Sir RALPH PAYNE-GALLWEY, Bart.
Vol. I. Field and Covert. With 105 Illustrations. Crown 8vo. 10s. 6d.
Vol. II. Moor and Marsh. With 65 Illustrations. Crown 8vo. 10s. 6d.

CYCLING. By VISCOUNT BURY (Earl of Albemarle) and G. LACY HILLIER. With 89 Illustrations. Crown 8vo. 10s. 6d.

ATHLETICS AND FOOTBALL. By MONTAGUE SHEARMAN. With 41 Illustrations. Crown 8vo. 10s. 6d.

BOATING. By W. B. WOODGATE. With 49 Illustrations. Crown 8vo. 10s. 6d.

CRICKET. By A. G. STEEL and the Hon. R. H. LYTTELTON. With 63 Illustrations. Crown 8vo. 10s. 6d.

DRIVING. By the DUKE OF BEAUFORT. With 65 Illustrations. Crown 8vo. 10s. 6d.

[*Continued.*

BADMINTON LIBRARY (The)—*(continued)*.

FENCING, BOXING, AND WRESTLING. By WALTER H. POLLOCK, F. C. GROVE, C. PREVOST, E. B. MICHELL, and WALTER ARMSTRONG. With 42 Illustrations. Crown 8vo. 10s. 6d.

GOLF. By HORACE HUTCHINSON, the Rt. Hon. A. J. BALFOUR, M.P., ANDREW LANG, Sir W. G. SIMPSON, Bart., &c. With 88 Illustrations. Crown 8vo. 10s. 6d.

TENNIS, LAWN TENNIS, RACKETS, AND FIVES. By J. M. and C. G. HEATHCOTE, E. O. PLEYDELL-BOUVERIE, and A. C. AINGER. With 79 Illustrations. Crown 8vo. 10s. 6d.

RIDING AND POLO. By Captain ROBERT WEIR, Riding-Master, R.H.G., J. MORAY BROWN, &c. With 59 Illustrations. Crown 8vo. 10s. 6d.

BAGEHOT (Walter).—BIOGRAPHICAL STUDIES. 8vo. 12s.

———— ECONOMIC STUDIES. 8vo. 10s. 6d.

———— LITERARY STUDIES. 2 vols. 8vo. 28s.

———— THE POSTULATES OF ENGLISH POLITICAL ECONOMY. Crown 8vo. 2s. 6d.

———— A PRACTICAL PLAN FOR ASSIMILATING THE ENGLISH AND AMERICAN MONEY AS A STEP TOWARDS A UNIVERSAL MONEY. Crown 8vo. 2s. 6d.

BAGWELL (Richard).—IRELAND UNDER THE TUDORS. (3 vols.) Vols. I. and II. From the first invasion of the Northmen to the year 1578. 8vo. 32s.   Vol. III. 1578-1603. 8vo. 18s.

BAIN (Alex.).—MENTAL AND MORAL SCIENCE. Crown 8vo. 10s. 6d.

———— SENSES AND THE INTELLECT. 8vo. 15s.

———— EMOTIONS AND THE WILL. 8vo. 15s.

———— LOGIC, DEDUCTIVE AND INDUCTIVE. Part I., *Deduction*, 4s. Part II., *Induction*, 6s. 6d.

———— PRACTICAL ESSAYS. Crown 8vo. 2s.

BAKER (James).—BY THE WESTERN SEA: a Novel. Cr. 8vo. 3s. 6d.

BAKER.—EIGHT YEARS IN CEYLON. With 6 Illustrations. Crown 8vo. 3s. 6d.

———— THE RIFLE AND THE HOUND IN CEYLON. With 6 Illustrations. Crown 8vo. 3s. 6d.

BALL (The Rt. Hon. T. J.).—THE REFORMED CHURCH OF IRELAND (1537-1889). 8vo. 7s. 6d.

———— HISTORICAL REVIEW OF THE LEGISLATIVE SYSTEMS OPERATIVE IN IRELAND (1172-1800). 8vo. 6s.

BEACONSFIELD (The Earl of).—NOVELS AND TALES. The Hughenden Edition. With 2 Portraits and 11 Vignettes. 11 vols. Crown 8vo. 42s.

Endymion.	Venetia.	Alroy, Ixion, &c.
Lothair.	Henrietta Temple.	The Young Duke, &c.
Coningsby.	Contarini Fleming, &c.	Vivian Grey.
Tancred. Sybil.		

NOVELS AND TALES. Cheap Edition. 11 vols. Crown 8vo. 1s. each, boards; 1s. 6d. each, cloth.

BECKER (Professor).—GALLUS; or, Roman Scenes in the Time of Augustus. Post 8vo. 7s. 6d.

———— CHARICLES ; or, Illustrations of the Private Life of the Ancient Greeks Post 8vo. 7s. 6d.

BELL (Mrs. Hugh).—WILL O' THE WISP : a Story. Crown 8vo. 3s. 6d.

———— CHAMBER COMEDIES. Crown 8vo. 6s.

BLAKE (J.).—TABLES FOR THE CONVERSION OF 5 PER CENT. INTEREST FROM $\frac{1}{16}$ TO 7 PER CENT. 8vo. 12s. 6d.

BOOK (THE) OF WEDDING DAYS. Arranged on the Plan of a Birthday Book. With 96 Illustrated Borders, Frontispiece, and Title-page by Walter Crane ; and Quotations for each Day. Compiled and Arranged by K. E. J. REID, MAY ROSS, and MABEL BAMFIELD. 4to. 21s.

BRASSEY (Lady).—A VOYAGE IN THE 'SUNBEAM,' OUR HOME ON THE OCEAN FOR ELEVEN MONTHS.

Library Edition. With 8 Maps and Charts, and 118 Illustrations, 8vo. 21s.
Cabinet Edition. With Map and 66 Illustrations, Crown 8vo. 7s. 6d.
Cheap Edition. With 66 Illustrations, Crown 8vo. 3s. 6d.
School Edition. With 37 Illustrations, Fcp. 2s. cloth, or 3s. white parchment.
Popular Edition. With 60 Illustrations, 4to. 6d. sewed, 1s. cloth.

———— SUNSHINE AND STORM IN THE EAST.

Library Edition. With 2 Maps and 114 Illustrations, 8vo. 21s.
Cabinet Edition. With 2 Maps and 114 Illustrations, Crown 8vo. 7s. 6d.
Popular Edition. With 103 Illustrations, 4to. 6d. sewed, 1s. cloth.

———— IN THE TRADES, THE TROPICS, AND THE 'ROARING FORTIES'.

Cabinet Edition. With Map and 220 Illustrations, Crown 8vo. 7s. 6d.
Popular Edition. With 183 Illustrations, 4to. 6d. sewed, 1s. cloth.

———— THE LAST VOYAGE TO INDIA AND AUSTRALIA IN THE 'SUNBEAM'. With Charts and Maps, and 40 Illustrations in Monotone (20 full-page), and nearly 200 Illustrations in the Text. 8vo. 21s.

———— THREE VOYAGES IN THE 'SUNBEAM'. Popular Edition. With 346 Illustrations, 4to. 2s. 6d.

BRAY (Charles).—THE PHILOSOPHY OF NECESSITY ; or, Law in Mind as in Matter. Crown 8vo. 5s.

BRIGHT (Rev. J. Franck).—A HISTORY OF ENGLAND. 4 vols. Cr. 8vo.
Period I.—Mediæval Monarchy : The Departure of the Romans to Richard III. From A.D. 449 to 1485. 4s. 6d.
Period II.—Personal Monarchy : Henry VII. to James II. From 1485 to 1688. 5s.
Period III.—Constitutional Monarchy : William and Mary to William IV. From 1689 to 1837. 7s. 6d.
Period IV.—The Growth of Democracy : Victoria. From 1837 to 1880. 6s.

BRYDEN (H. A.).—KLOOF AND KARROO : Sport, Legend, and Natural History in Cape Colony. With 17 Illustrations. 8vo. 10s. 6d.

BUCKLE (Henry Thomas).—HISTORY OF CIVILISATION IN ENGLAND AND FRANCE, SPAIN AND SCOTLAND. 3 vols. Cr. 8vo. 24s.

BULL (Thomas).—HINTS TO MOTHERS ON THE MANAGEMENT OF THEIR HEALTH during the Period of Pregnancy. Fcp. 8vo. 1s. 6d.
———— THE MATERNAL MANAGEMENT OF CHILDREN IN HEALTH AND DISEASE. Fcp. 8vo. 1s. 6d.

BUTLER (Samuel).—EREWHON. Crown 8vo. 5s.
———— THE FAIR HAVEN. A Work in Defence of the Miraculous Element in our Lord's Ministry. Crown 8vo. 7s. 6d.
———— LIFE AND HABIT. An Essay after a Completer View of Evolution. Cr. 8vo. 7s. 6d.
———— EVOLUTION, OLD AND NEW. Crown 8vo. 10s. 6d.
———— UNCONSCIOUS MEMORY. Crown 8vo. 7s. 6d.
———— ALPS AND SANCTUARIES OF PIEDMONT AND THE CANTON TICINO. Illustrated. Pott 4to. 10s. 6d.
———— SELECTIONS FROM WORKS. Crown 8vo. 7s. 6d.
———— LUCK, OR CUNNING, AS THE MAIN MEANS OF ORGANIC MODIFICATION? Crown 8vo. 7s. 6d.
———— EX VOTO. An Account of the Sacro Monte or New Jerusalem at Varallo-Sesia. Crown 8vo. 10s. 6d.
———— HOLBEIN'S 'LA DANSE'. 3s.

CARLYLE (Thomas).—THOMAS CARLYLE: a History of his Life. By J. A. Froude. 1795-1835, 2 vols. Cr. 8vo. 7s. 1834-1881, 2 vols. Cr. 8vo. 7s.

CASE (Thomas).—PHYSICAL REALISM : being an Analytical Philosophy from the Physical Objects of Science to the Physical Data of Sense. 8vo. 15s.

CHETWYND (Sir George).—RACING REMINISCENCES AND EXPERIENCES OF THE TURF. 2 vols. 8vo. 21s.

CHILD (Gilbert W.).—CHURCH AND STATE UNDER THE TUDORS. 8vo. 15s.

CHISHOLM (G. G.).—HANDBOOK OF COMMERCIAL GEOGRAPHY. With 29 Maps. 8vo. 16s.

CHURCH (Sir Richard).—Commander-in-Chief of the Greeks in the War of Independence : a Memoir. By Stanley Lane-Poole. 8vo. 5s.

CLIVE (Mrs. Archer).—POEMS. Including the IX. Poems. Fcp. 8vo. 6s.

CLODD (Edward).—THE STORY OF CREATION : a Plain Account of Evolution. With 77 Illustrations. Crown 8vo. 3s. 6d.

CLUTTERBUCK (W. J.).—THE SKIPPER IN ARCTIC SEAS. With 39 Illustrations. Crown 8vo. 10s. 6d.
———— ABOUT CEYLON AND BORNEO : being an Account of Two Visits to Ceylon, one to Borneo, and How we Fell Out on our Homeward Journey. With 47 Illustrations. Crown 8vo.

COLENSO (J. W.).—THE PENTATEUCH AND BOOK OF JOSHUA CRITICALLY EXAMINED. Crown 8vo. 6s.

COMYN (L. N.).—ATHERSTONE PRIORY : a Tale. Crown 8vo. 2s. 6d.

CONINGTON (John).—THE ÆNEID OF VIRGIL. Translated into English Verse. Crown 8vo. 6s.
———— THE POEMS OF VIRGIL. Translated into English Prose. Cr. 8vo. 6s.

COX (Rev. Sir G. W.).—A HISTORY OF GREECE, from the Earliest Period to the Death of Alexander the Great. With 11 Maps. Cr. 8vo. 7s. 6d.

CRAKE (Rev. A. D.).—HISTORICAL TALES. Cr. 8vo. 5 vols. 2s. 6d. each.

Edwy the Fair; or, The First Chronicle of Æscendune.	**The House of Walderne.** A Tale of ·the Cloister and the Forest in the Days of the Barons' Wars.
Alfgar the Dane; or, The Second Chronicle of Æscendune.	**Brain Fitz-Count.** A Story of Wallingford Castle and Dorchester Abbey.
The Rival Heirs: being the Third and Last Chronicle of Æscendune.	

———— HISTORY OF THE CHURCH UNDER THE ROMAN EMPIRE, A.D. 30-476. Crown 8vo. 7s. 6d.

CREIGHTON (Mandell, D.D.)—HISTORY OF THE PAPACY DURING THE REFORMATION. 8vo. Vols. I. and II., 1378-1464, 32s. ; Vols. III. and IV., 1464-1518, 24s.

CRUMP (A.).—A SHORT ENQUIRY INTO THE FORMATION OF POLITICAL OPINION, from the Reign of the Great Families to the Advent of Democracy. 8vo. 7s. 6d.

———— AN INVESTIGATION INTO THE CAUSES OF THE GREAT FALL IN PRICES which took place coincidently with the Demonetisation of Silver by Germany. 8vo. 6s.

CURZON (Hon. George N.).—RUSSIA IN CENTRAL ASIA IN 1889 AND THE ANGLO-RUSSIAN QUESTION. 8vo. 21s.

DANTE.—LA COMMEDIA DI DANTE. A New Text, carefully Revised with the aid of the most recent Editions and Collations. Small 8vo. 6s.

DE LA SAUSSAYE (Prof. Chantepie).—A MANUAL OF THE SCIENCE OF RELIGION. Translated by Mrs. COLYER FERGUSSON (*née* MAX MÜLLER). Crown 8vo. 12s. 6d.

DELAND (Mrs.).—JOHN WARD, PREACHER. Cr. 8vo. 2s. bds., 2s. 6d. cl.

———— SIDNEY: a Novel. Crown 8vo. 6s.

———— THE OLD GARDEN, and other Verses. Fcp. 8vo. 5s.

DE REDCLIFFE.—THE LIFE OF THE RIGHT HON. STRATFORD CANNING : VISCOUNT STRATFORD DE REDCLIFFE. By STANLEY LANE-POOLE. With 3 Portraits. Crown 8vo. 7s. 6d.

DE SALIS (Mrs.).—Works by :—

Cakes and Confections à la Mode. Fcp. 8vo. 1s. 6d.	**Puddings and Pastry à la Mode.** Fcp. 8vo. 1s. 6d.
Dressed Game and Poultry à la Mode. Fcp. 8vo. 1s. 6d.	**Savouries à la Mode.** Fcp. 8vo. 1s. 6d.
Dressed Vegetables à la Mode. Fcp. 8vo. 1s. 6d.	**Soups and Dressed Fish à la Mode.** Fcp. 8vo. 1s. 6d.
Drinks à la Mode. Fcp. 8vo. 1s. 6d.	**Sweets and Supper Dishes à la Mode.** Fcp. 8vo. 1s. 6d.
Entrées à la Mode. Fcp. 1s. 8vo. 6d.	**Tempting Dishes for Small Incomes.** Fcp. 8vo. 1s. 6d.
Floral Decorations. Fcp. 8vo. 1s. 6d.	**Wrinkles and Notions for every Household.** Crown 8vo. 2s. 6d.
Oysters à la Mode. Fcp. 8vo. 1s. 6d.	

DE TOCQUEVILLE (Alexis).—DEMOCRACY IN AMERICA. Translated by HENRY REEVE, C.B. 2 vols. Crown 8vo. 16s.

DOWELL (Stephen).—A HISTORY OF TAXATION AND TAXES IN ENGLAND. 4 vols. 8vo. Vols. I. and II., The History of Taxation, 21s. Vols. III. and IV., The History of Taxes, 21s.

DOYLE (A. Conan).—MICAH CLARKE : a Tale of Monmouth's Rebellion. With Frontispiece and Vignette. Crown 8vo. 3s. 6d.

———— THE CAPTAIN OF THE POLESTAR ; and other Tales. Cr. 8vo. 6s.

DRANE (Augusta T.).—THE HISTORY OF ST. DOMINIC, FOUNDER OF THE FRIAR PREACHERS. With 32 Illustrations. 8vo. 15s.

DUBLIN UNIVERSITY PRESS SERIES (The): a Series of Works undertaken by the Provost and Senior Fellows of Trinity College, Dublin.

Abbott's (T. K.) Codex Rescriptus Dublinensis of St. Matthew. 4to. 21s.
——— Evangeliorum Versio Antehieronymiana ex Codice Usseriano (Dublinensi). 2 vols. Cr. 8vo. 21s.

Allman's (G. J.) Greek Geometry from Thales to Euclid. 8vo. 10s. 6d.

Burnside (W. S.) and Panton's (A. W.) Theory of Equations. 8vo. 12s. 6d.

Casey's (John) Sequel to Euclid's Elements. Crown 8vo. 3s. 6d.
——— Analytical Geometry of the Conic Sections. Crown 8vo. 7s. 6d.

Davies' (J. F.) Eumenides of Æschylus. With Metrical English Translation. 8vo. 7s.

Dublin Translations into Greek and Latin Verse. Edited by R. Y. Tyrrell. 8vo. 6s.

Graves' (R. P.) Life of Sir William Hamilton. 3 vols. 15s. each.

Griffin (R. W.) on Parabola, Ellipse, and Hyperbola. Crown 8vo. 6s.

Hobart's (W. K.) Medical Language of St. Luke. 8vo. 16s.

Leslie's (T. E. Cliffe) Essays in Political Economy. 8vo. 10s. 6d.

Macalister's (A.) Zoology and Morphology of Vertebrata. 8vo. 10s. 6d.

MacCullagh's (James) Mathematical and other Tracts. 8vo. 15s.

Maguire's (T.) Parmenides of Plato, Text with Introduction, Analysis, &c. 8vo. 7s. 6d.

Monck's (W. H. S.) Introduction to Logic. Crown 8vo. 5s.

Roberts' (R. A.) Examples on the Analytic Geometry of Plane Conics. Crown 8vo. 5s.

Southey's (R.) Correspondence with Caroline Bowles. Edited by E. Dowden. 8vo. 14s.

Stubbs' (J. W.) History of the University of Dublin, from its Foundation to the End of the Eighteenth Century. 8vo. 12s. 6d.

Thornhill's (W. J.) The Æneid of Virgil, freely translated into English Blank Verse. Crown 8vo. 7s. 6d.

Tyrrell's (R. Y.) Cicero's Correspondence.
Vols. I., II. and III. 8vo. each 12s.
——— The Acharnians of Aristophanes, translated into English Verse. Crown 8vo. 1s.

Webb's (T. E.) Goethe's Faust, Translation and Notes. 8vo. 12s. 6d.
——— The Veil of Isis; a Series of Essays on Idealism. 8vo. 10s. 6d.

Wilkins' (G.) The Growth of the Homeric Poems. 8vo. 6s.

EWALD (Heinrich).—THE ANTIQUITIES OF ISRAEL. 8vo. 12s. 6d.

——— THE HISTORY OF ISRAEL. 8vo. Vols. I. and II. 24s. Vols. III. and IV. 21s. Vol. V. 18s. Vol. VI. 16s. Vol. VII. 21s. Vol. VIII. 18s.

FARNELL (G. S.).—THE GREEK LYRIC POETS. 8vo. 16s.

FARRAR (F. W.).—LANGUAGE AND LANGUAGES. Crown 8vo. 6s.

——— DARKNESS AND DAWN; or, Scenes in the Days of Nero. An Historic Tale. 2 vols. 8vo. 28s.

FIRTH (J. C.).—NATION MAKING: a Story of New Zealand Savageism and Civilisation. Crown 8vo. 6s.

FITZWYGRAM (Major-General Sir F.).—HORSES AND STABLES. With 19 pages of Illustrations. 8vo. 5s.

FORD (Horace).—THE THEORY AND PRACTICE OF ARCHERY. New Edition, thoroughly Revised and Re-written by W. BUTT. 8vo. 14s.

FOUARD (Abbé Constant).—THE CHRIST THE SON OF GOD. With Introduction by Cardinal Manning. 2 vols. Crown 8vo. 14s.

Missing Page

GWILT (Joseph).—AN ENCYCLOPÆDIA OF ARCHITECTURE. With more than 1700 Engravings on Wood. 8vo. 52s. 6d.

HAGGARD (Ella).—LIFE AND ITS AUTHOR: an Essay in Verse. With a Memoir by H. Rider Haggard, and Portrait. Fcp. 8vo. 3s. 6d.

HAGGARD (H. Rider).—SHE. With 32 Illustrations. Crown 8vo. 3s. 6d.
———— ALLAN QUATERMAIN. With 31 Illustrations. Crown 8vo. 3s. 6d.
———— MAIWA'S REVENGE. Crown 8vo. 1s. boards, 1s. 6d. cloth.
———— COLONEL QUARITCH, V.C. Crown 8vo. 3s. 6d.
———— CLEOPATRA: With 29 Illustrations. Crown 8vo. 3s. 6d.
———— BEATRICE. Crown 8vo. 6s.
———— ERIC BRIGHTEYES. With 51 Illustrations. Crown 8vo. 6s.

HAGGARD (H. Rider) and LANG (Andrew).—THE WORLD'S DESIRE. Crown 8vo. 6s.

HALLIWELL-PHILLIPPS (J. O.)—A CALENDAR OF THE HALLI-WELL-PHILLIPPS COLLECTION OF SHAKESPEAREAN RARITIES. Second Edition. Enlarged by Ernest E. Baker. 8vo. 10s. 6d.
———— OUTLINE OF THE LIFE OF SHAKESPEARE. 2 vols. Royal 8vo. 21s.

HARRISON (Jane E.).—MYTHS OF THE ODYSSEY IN ART AND LITERATURE. Illustrated with Outline Drawings. 8vo. 18s.

HARRISON (F. Bayford).—THE CONTEMPORARY HISTORY OF THE FRENCH REVOLUTION. Crown 8vo. 3s. 6d.

HARTE (Bret).—IN THE CARQUINEZ WOODS. Fcp. 8vo. 1s. bds., 1s. 6d. cloth.
———— BY SHORE AND SEDGE. 16mo. 1s.
———— ON THE FRONTIER. 16mo. 1s.

HARTWIG (Dr.).—THE SEA AND ITS LIVING WONDERS. With 12 Plates and 303 Woodcuts. 8vo. 10s. 6d.
THE TROPICAL WORLD. With 8 Plates and 172 Woodcuts. 8vo. 10s. 6d.
THE POLAR WORLD. With 3 Maps, 8 Plates and 85 Woodcuts. 8vo. 10s. 6d.
THE SUBTERRANEAN WORLD. With 3 Maps and 80 Woodcuts. 8vo. 10s. 6d.
THE AERIAL WORLD. With Map, 8 Plates and 60 Woodcuts. 8vo. 10s. 6d.

HAVELOCK.—MEMOIRS OF SIR HENRY HAVELOCK, K.C.B. By JOHN CLARK MARSHMAN. Crown 8vo. 3s. 6d.

HEARN (W. Edward).—THE GOVERNMENT OF ENGLAND: its Structure and its Development. 8vo. 16s.
———— THE ARYAN HOUSEHOLD: its Structure and ts Development. An Introduction to Comparative Jurisprudence. 8vo. 16s.

HISTORIC TOWNS. Edited by E. A. FREEMAN and Rev. WILLIAM HUNT. With Maps and Plans. Crown 8vo. 3s. 6d. each.

Bristol. By Rev. W. Hunt.	**Winchester.** By Rev. G. W. Kitchin.
Carlisle. By Dr. Mandell Creighton.	**New York.** By Theodore Roosevelt.
Cinque Ports. By Montagu Burrows.	**Boston (U.S.).** By Henry Cabot Lodge.
Colchester. By Rev. E. L. Cutts.	
Exeter. By E. A. Freeman.	**York.** By Rev. James Raine.
London. By Rev. W. J. Loftie.	[*In preparation.*
Oxford. By Rev. C. W. Boase.	

HODGSON (Shadworth H.).—TIME AND SPACE: a Metaphysical Essay. 8vo. 16s.

———— THE THEORY OF PRACTICE: an Ethical Enquiry. 2 vols. 8vo. 24s.

———— THE PHILOSOPHY OF REFLECTION. 2 vols. 8vo. 21s.

———— OUTCAST ESSAYS AND VERSE TRANSLATIONS. Crown 8vo. 8s. 6d.

HOWITT (William).—VISITS TO REMARKABLE PLACES. 80 Illustrations. Crown 8vo. 3s. 6d.

HULLAH (John).—COURSE OF LECTURES ON THE HISTORY OF MODERN MUSIC. 8vo. 8s. 6d.

———— COURSE OF LECTURES ON THE TRANSITION PERIOD OF MUSICAL HISTORY. 8vo. 10s. 6d.

HUME.—THE PHILOSOPHICAL WORKS OF DAVID HUME. Edited by T. H. GREEN and T. H. GROSE. 4 vols. 8vo. 56s.

HUTCHINSON (Horace).—CREATURES OF CIRCUMSTANCE: a Novel. 3 vols. Crown 8vo. 25s. 6d.

———— FAMOUS GOLF LINKS. By HORACE G. HUTCHINSON, ANDREW LANG, H. S. C. EVERARD, T. RUTHERFORD CLARK, &c. With numerous Illustrations by F. P. Hopkins, T. Hodges, H. S. King, &c. Crown 8vo. 6s.

HUTH (Alfred H.).—THE MARRIAGE OF NEAR KIN. Royal 8vo. 21s.

INGELOW (Jean).—POETICAL WORKS. Vols. I. and II. Fcp. 8vo. 12s. Vol. III. Fcp. 8vo. 5s.

———— LYRICAL AND OTHER POEMS. Selected from the Writings of JEAN INGELOW. Fcp. 8vo. 2s. 6d. cloth plain, 3s. cloth gilt.

———— VERY YOUNG and QUITE ANOTHER STORY: Two Stories. Crown 8vo. 6s.

JAMESON (Mrs.).—SACRED AND LEGENDARY ART. With 19 Etchings and 187 Woodcuts. 2 vols. 8vo. 20s. net.

———— LEGENDS OF THE MADONNA, the Virgin Mary as represented in Sacred and Legendary Art. With 27 Etchings and 165 Woodcuts. 8vo. 10s. net.

———— LEGENDS OF THE MONASTIC ORDERS. With 11 Etchings and 88 Woodcuts. 8vo. 10s. net.

———— HISTORY OF OUR LORD. His Types and Precursors. Completed by LADY EASTLAKE. With 31 Etchings and 281 Woodcuts. 2 vols. 8vo. 20s. net.

JEFFERIES (Richard).—FIELD AND HEDGEROW. Last Essays. Crown 8vo. 3s. 6d.

———— THE STORY OF MY HEART: My Autobiography. Crown 8vo. 3s. 6d.

JENNINGS (Rev. A. C.).—ECCLESIA ANGLICANA. A History of the Church of Christ in England. Crown 8vo. 7s. 6d.

JESSOP (G. H.).—JUDGE LYNCH: a Tale of the California Vineyards. Crown 8vo. 6s.

JOHNSON (J. & J. H.).—THE PATENTEE'S MANUAL; a Treatise on the Law and Practice of Letters Patent. 8vo. 10s. 6d.

JORDAN (William Leighton).—THE STANDARD OF VALUE. 8vo. 6s.

JUSTINIAN.—THE INSTITUTES OF JUSTINIAN; Latin Text, with English Introduction, &c. By THOMAS C. SANDARS. 8vo. 18s.

KALISCH (M. M.).—BIBLE STUDIES. Part I. The Prophecies of Balaam. 8vo. 10s. 6d. Part II. The Book of Jonah. 8vo. 10s. 6d.

KALISCH (M. M.).—COMMENTARY ON THE OLD TESTAMENT; with a New Translation. Vol. I. Genesis, 8vo. 18s., or adapted for the General Reader, 12s. Vol. II. Exodus, 15s., or adapted for the General Reader, 12s. Vol. III. Leviticus, Part I. 15s., or adapted for the General Reader, 8s. Vol. IV. Leviticus, Part II. 15s., or adapted for the General Reader, 8s.

KANT (Immanuel).—CRITIQUE OF PRACTICAL REASON, AND OTHER WORKS ON THE THEORY OF ETHICS. 8vo. 12s. 6d.

———— INTRODUCTION TO LOGIC. Translated by T. K. Abbott. Notes by S. T. Coleridge. 8vo. 6s.

KENNEDY (Arthur Clark).—PICTURES IN RHYME. With 4 Illustrations by Maurice Greiffenhagen. Crown 8vo. 6s.

KILLICK (Rev. A. H.).—HANDBOOK TO MILL'S SYSTEM OF LOGIC. Crown 8vo. 3s. 6d.

KNIGHT (E. F.).—THE CRUISE OF THE 'ALERTE'; the Narrative of a Search for Treasure on the Desert Island of Trinidad. With 2 Maps and 23 Illustrations. Crown 8vo. 10s. 6d.

———— SAVE ME FROM MY FRIENDS: a Novel. Crown 8vo. 6s.

LADD (George T.).—ELEMENTS OF PHYSIOLOGICAL PSYCHO-LOGY. 8vo. 21s.

———— OUTLINES OF PHYSIOLOGICAL PSYCHOLOGY. A Text-Book of Mental Science for Academies and Colleges. 8vo. 12s.

LANG (Andrew).—CUSTOM AND MYTH: Studies of Early Usage and Belief. With 15 Illustrations. Crown 8vo. 7s. 6d.

———— BOOKS AND BOOKMEN. With 2 Coloured Plates and 17 Illustrations. Crown 8vo. 6s. 6d.

———— GRASS OF PARNASSUS. A Volume of Selected Verses. Fcp. 8vo. 6s.

———— BALLADS OF BOOKS. Edited by ANDREW LANG. Fcp. 8vo. 6s.

———— THE BLUE FAIRY BOOK. Edited by ANDREW LANG. With 8 Plates and 130 Illustrations in the Text. Crown 8vo. 6s.

———— THE RED FAIRY BOOK. Edited by ANDREW LANG. With 4 Plates and 96 Illustrations in the Text. Crown 8vo. 6s.

———— THE BLUE POETRY BOOK. With 12 Plates and 88 Illustrations in the Text. Crown 8vo. 6s.

———— ANGLING SKETCHES. With Illustrations by W. G. BURN-MURDOCH. Crown 8vo. 7s. 6d.

LAVISSE (Ernest).—GENERAL VIEW OF THE POLITICAL HIS-TORY OF EUROPE.

LAYARD (Nina F.).—POEMS. Crown 8vo. 6s.

LECKY (W. E. H.).—HISTORY OF ENGLAND IN THE EIGHTEENTH CENTURY. 8vo. Vols. I. and II. 1700-1760. 36s. Vols. III. and IV. 1760-1784. 36s. Vols. V. and VI. 1784-1793. 36s. Vols. VII. and VIII. 1793-1800. 36s.

———— THE HISTORY OF EUROPEAN MORALS FROM AUGUSTUS TO CHARLEMAGNE. 2 vols. Crown 8vo. 16s.

———— HISTORY OF THE RISE AND INFLUENCE OF THE SPIRIT OF RATIONALISM IN EUROPE. 2 vols. Crown 8vo. 16s.

———— POEMS. Fcap. 8vo. 5s.

LEES (J. A.) and CLUTTERBUCK (W. J.).—B.C. 1887, A RAMBLE IN BRITISH COLUMBIA. With Map and 75 Illustrations. Cr. 8vo. 6s.

LEGER (Louis).—A HISTORY OF AUSTRO-HUNGARY. From the Earliest Time to the year 1889. With Preface by E. A. Freeman. Cr. 8vo. 10s. 6d.

LEWES (George Henry).—THE HISTORY OF PHILOSOPHY, from Thales to Comte. 2 vo s. 8vo. 32s.

LIDDELL (Colonel R. T.).—MEMOIRS OF THE TENTH ROYAL HUSSARS. With Numerous Illustrations. 2 vols. Imperial 8vo. 63s.

LONGMAN (Frederick W.).—CHESS OPENINGS. Fcp. 8vo. 2s. 6d.

———— FREDERICK THE GREAT AND THE SEVEN YEARS' WAR. Fcp. 8vo. 2s. 6d.

LONGMORE (Sir T.).—RICHARD WISEMAN, Surgeon and Sergeant-Surgeon to Charles II. A Biographical Study. With Portrait.

LOUDON (J. C.).—ENCYCLOPÆDIA OF GARDENING. With 1000 Woodcuts. 8vo. 21s.

———— ENCYCLOPÆDIA OF AGRICULTURE; the Laying-out, Improvement, and Management of Landed Property. With 1100 Woodcuts. 8vo. 21s.

———— ENCYCLOPÆDIA OF PLANTS; the Specific Character, &c., of all Plants found in Great Britain. With 12,000 Woodcuts. 8vo. 42s.

LUBBOCK (Sir J.).—THE ORIGIN OF CIVILISATION and the Primitive Condition of Man. With 5 Plates and 20 Illustrations in the Text. 8vo. 18s.

LYALL (Edna).—THE AUTOBIOGRAPHY OF A SLANDER. Fcp. 8vo. 1s. sewed.

LYDE (Lionel W.).—AN INTRODUCTION TO ANCIENT HISTORY. With 3 Coloured Maps. Crown 8vo. 3s.

MACAULAY (Lord).—COMPLETE WORKS OF LORD MACAULAY.

Library Edition, 8 vols. 8vo. £5 5s.	Cabinet Edition, 16 vols. post 8vo. £4 16s.

———— HISTORY OF ENGLAND FROM THE ACCESSION OF JAMES THE SECOND.

Popular Edition, 2 vols. Crown 8vo. 5s.	People's Edition, 4 vols. Crown 8vo. 16s.
Student's Edition, 2 vols. Crown 8vo. 12s.	Cabinet Edition, 8 vols. Post 8vo. 48s.
	Library Edition, 5 vols. 8vo. £4.

———— CRITICAL AND HISTORICAL ESSAYS, WITH LAYS OF ANCIENT ROME, in 1 volume.

Popular Edition, Crown 8vo. 2s. 6d.	Authorised Edition, Crown 8vo. 2s. 6d., or 3s. 6d. gilt edges.

[Continued.

MACAULAY (Lord).—ESSAYS (*continued*).

———— CRITICAL AND HISTORICAL ESSAYS.

Student's Edition.   Crown 8vo. 6s. | Trevelyan Edition, 2 vols. Crown 8vo.9s.
People's Edition, 2 vols. Crown 8vo. 8s. | Cabinet Edition, 4 vols. Post 8vo. 24s.
| Library Edition, 3 vols. 8vo. 36s.

———— ESSAYS which may be had separately, price 6d. each sewed. 1s. each cloth.

Addison and Walpole. | **Ranke and Gladstone.**
Frederic the Great. | **Milton and Machiavelli.**
Croker's Boswell's Johnson. | **Lord Bacon.**
Hallam's Constitutional History. | **Lord Clive.**
Warren Hastings(3d. sewed, 6d. cloth). | **Lord Byron, and the Comic Drama-**
The Earl of Chatham (Two Essays). | **tists of the Restoration.**

The Essay on Warren Hastings, anno- | **The Essay on Lord Clive,** annotated by
tated by S. Hales. Fcp. 8vo. 1s. 6d. | H.Courthope Bowen. Fcp.8vo.2s.6d.

———— SPEECHES. People's Edition, Crown 8vo. 3s. 6d.

———— LAYS OF ANCIENT ROME, &c. Illustrated by G. Scharf. Library
Edition. Fcp. 4to. 10s. 6d.

Bijou Edition, 18mo. 2s. 6d. gilt top. | Popular Edition, Fcp. 4to. 6d. sewed,
| 1s. cloth.

———————————————— Illustrated by J. R. Weguelin.   Crown

8vo. 3s. 6d. gilt edges.

———————————————— Annotated Edition, Fcp.8vo. 1s. sewed,
Cabinet Edition, Post 8vo. 3s. 6d. | 1s. 6d. cloth.

———— MISCELLANEOUS WRITINGS.

People's Edition.   Crown 8vo. 4s. 6d. | Library Edition, 2 vols. 8vo. 21s.

———— MISCELLANEOUS WRITINGS AND SPEECHES.

Popular Edition.   Crown 8vo. 2s. 6d. | Cabinet Edition, Post 8vo. 24s.
Student's Edition.   Crown 8vo. 6s. |

———— SELECTIONS FROM THE WRITINGS OF LORD MACAULAY.
Edited, with Notes, by the Right Hon. Sir G. O. TREVELYAN. Crown 8vo. 6s.

———— THE LIFE AND LETTERS OF LORD MACAULAY. By the Right
Hon. Sir G. O. TREVELYAN.

Popular Edition.   Crown. 8vo. 2s. 6d. | Cabinet Edition, 2 vols. Post 8vo. 12s.
Student's Edition.   Crown 8vo. 6s. | Library Edition, 2 vols. 8vo. 36s.

MACDONALD (George).—UNSPOKEN SERMONS.   Three Series.
Crown 8vo. 3s. 6d. each.

———— THE MIRACLES OF OUR LORD. Crown 8vo. 3s. 6d.

———— A BOOK OF STRIFE, IN THE FORM OF THE DIARY OF AN
OLD SOUL : Poems. 12mo. 6s.

MACFARREN (Sir G. A.).—LECTURES ON HARMONY. 8vo. 12s.

———— ADDRESSES AND LECTURES. Crown 8vo. 6s. 6d.

MACKAIL (J. W.).—SELECT EPIGRAMS FROM THE GREEK AN-
THOLOGY. With a Revised Text, Introduction, Translation, &c. 8vo. 16s.

MACLEOD (Henry D.).—THE ELEMENTS OF BANKING. Crown
8vo. 3s. 6d.

———— THE THEORY AND PRACTICE OF BANKING. Vol. I. 8vo. 12s.,
Vol. II. 14s.

———— THE THEORY OF CREDIT. 8vo. Vol. I. [*New Edition in the Press*];
Vol. II. Part I. 4s. 6d. ; Vol. 1 . Part II. 10s. 6d.

McCULLOCH (J. R.).—THE DICTIONARY OF COMMERCE and Commercial Navigation. With 11 Maps and 30 Charts. 8vo. 63s.

MACVINE (John).—SIXTY-THREE YEARS' ANGLING, from the Mountain Streamlet to the Mighty Tay. Crown 8vo. 10s. 6d.

MALMESBURY (The Earl of).—MEMOIRS OF AN EX-MINISTER. Crown 8vo. 7s. 6d.

MANNERING (G. E.).—WITH AXE AND ROPE IN THE NEW ZEALAND ALPS. Illustrated. 8vo. 12s. 6d.

MANUALS OF CATHOLIC PHILOSOPHY (*Stonyhurst Series*).

Logic. By Richard F. Clarke. Crown 8vo. 5s.

First Principles of Knowledge. By John Rickaby. Crown 8vo. 5s.

Moral Philosophy (Ethics and Natural Law). By Joseph Rickaby. Crown 8vo. 5s.

General Metaphysics. By John Rickaby. Crown 8vo. 5s.

Psychology. By Michael Maher. Crown 8vo. 6s. 6d.

Natural Theology. By Bernard Boedder. Crown 8vo. 6s. 6d.

A Manual of Political Economy. By C. S. Devas. 6s. 6d. [*In preparation.*

MARTINEAU (James).—HOURS OF THOUGHT ON SACRED THINGS. Two Volumes of Sermons. 2 vols. Crown 8vo. 7s. 6d. each.

———— ENDEAVOURS AFTER THE CHRISTIAN LIFE. Discourses. Crown 8vo. 7s. 6d.

———— THE SEAT OF AUTHORITY IN RELIGION. 8vo. 14s.

———— ESSAYS, REVIEWS, AND ADDRESSES. 4 vols. Crown 8vo. 7s. 6d. each.

I. Personal · Political.
II. Ecclesiastical : Historical.

III. Theological : Philosophical.
IV. Academical : Religious.

MASON (Agnes).—THE STEPS OF THE SUN : Daily Readings of Prose. 16mo. 3s. 6d.

MAUNDER'S TREASURIES. Fcp. 8vo. 6s. each volume.

Biographical Treasury.

Treasury of Natural History. With 900 Woodcuts.

Treasury of Geography. With 7 Maps and 16 Plates.

Scientific and Literary Treasury.

Historical Treasury.

Treasury of Knowledge.

The Treasury of Bible Knowledge. By the Rev. J. AYRE. With 5 Maps, 15 Plates, and 300 Woodcuts. Fcp. 8vo. 6s.

The Treasury of Botany. Edited by J. LINDLEY and T. MOORE. With 274 Woodcuts and 20 Steel Plates. 2 vols.

MATTHEWS (Brander).—A FAMILY TREE, and other Stories. Crown 8vo. 6s.

———— PEN AND INK—School Papers. Crown 8vo. 5s.

———— WITH MY FRIENDS : Tales told in Partnership. Crown 8vo. 6s.

MAX MÜLLER (F.).—SELECTED ESSAYS ON LANGUAGE, MYTHOLOGY, AND RELIGION. 2 vols. Crown 8vo. 16s.

———— THREE LECTURES ON THE SCIENCE OF LANGUAGE. Cr. 8vo. 3s.

———— THE SCIENCE OF LANGUAGE, founded on Lectures delivered at the Royal Institution in 1861 and 1863. 2 vols. Crown 8vo. 21s.

———— HIBBERT LECTURES ON THE ORIGIN AND GROWTH OF RELIGION, as illustrated by the Religions of India. Crown 8vo. 7s. 6d.

[*Continued.*

MAX MÜLLER (F.)—INTRODUCTION TO THE SCIENCE OF RELIGION ; FourLectures delivered at the Royal Institution. Crown 8vo. 7s. 6d.

———— NATURAL RELIGION. The Gifford Lectures, delivered before the University of Glasgow in 1888. Crown 8vo. 10s. 6d.

———— PHYSICAL RELIGION. The Gifford Lectures, delivered before the University of Glasgow in 1890. Crown 8vo. 10s. 6d.

———— THE SCIENCE OF THOUGHT. 8vo. 21s.

———— THREE INTRODUCTORY LECTURES ON THE SCIENCE OF THOUGHT. 8vo. 2s. 6d.

———— BIOGRAPHIES OF WORDS, AND THE HOME OF THE ARYAS. Crown 8vo. 7s. 6d.

———— A SANSKRIT GRAMMAR FOR BEGINNERS. New and Abridged Edition. By A. A. MacDonell. Crown 8vo. 6s.

MAY (Sir Thomas Erskine).—THE CONSTITUTIONAL HISTORY OF ENGLAND since the Accession of George III. 3 vols. Crown 8vo. 18s.

MEADE (L. T.).—THE O'DONNELLS OF INCHFAWN. Crown 8vo. 6s.

———— DADDY'S BOY. With Illustrations. Crown 8vo. 5s.

———— DEB AND THE DUCHESS. Illustrated by M. E. Edwards. Cr. 8vo. 5s.

———— HOUSE OF SURPRISES. Illustrated by E. M. Scannell. Cr. 8vo. 3s. 6d.

———— THE BERESFORD PRIZE. Illustrated by M. E. Edwards. Cr. 8vo. 5s.

MEATH (The Earl of).—SOCIAL ARROWS : Reprinted Articles on various Social Subjects. Crown 8vo. 5s.

———— PROSPERITY OR PAUPERISM ? Physical, Industrial, and Technical Training. Edited by the Earl of Meath. 8vo. 5s.

MELVILLE (G. J. Whyte).—Novels by. Crown 8vo. 1s. each, boards : 1s. 6d. each, cloth.

The Gladiators.	**The Queen's Maries.**	**Digby Grand.**
The Interpreter.	**Holmby House.**	**General Bounce.**
Good for Nothing.	**Kate Coventry.**	

MENDELSSOHN.—THE LETTERS OF FELIX MENDELSSOHN. Translated by Lady Wallace. 2 vols. Crown 8vo. 10s.

MERIVALE (Rev. Chas.).—HISTORY OF THE ROMANS UNDER THE EMPIRE. Cabinet Edition, 8 vols. Crown 8vo. 48s. Popular Edition, 8 vols. Crown 8vo. 3s. 6d. each.

———— THE FALL OF THE ROMAN REPUBLIC : a Short History of the Last Century of the Commonwealth. 12mo. 7s. 6d.

———— GENERAL HISTORY OF ROME FROM B.C. 753 TO A.D. 476. Cr. 8vo. 7s. 6d.

———— THE ROMAN TRIUMVIRATES. With Maps. Fcp. 8vo. 2s. 6d.

MILES (W. A.).—THE CORRESPONDENCE OF WILLIAM AUGUSTUS MILES ON THE FRENCH REVOLUTION, 1789–1817. 2 vols. 8vo. 32s.

MILL (James).—ANALYSIS OF THE PHENOMENA OF THE HUMAN MIND. 2 vols. 8vo. 28s.

MILL (John Stuart).—PRINCIPLES OF POLITICAL ECONOMY. Library Edition, 2 vols. 8vo. 30s. | People's Edition, 1 vol. Crown 8vo. 3s. 6d.

———— A SYSTEM OF LOGIC. Crown 8vo. 3s. 6d.

———— ON LIBERTY. Crown 8vo. 1s. 4d. *[Continued.*

MILL (J. S.).—ON REPRESENTATIVE GOVERNMENT. Crown 8vo. 2s.

——— UTILITARIANISM. 8vo. 5s.

——— EXAMINATION OF SIR WILLIAM HAMILTON'S PHILO-SOPHY. 8vo. 16s.

——— NATURE, THE UTILITY OF RELIGION AND THEISM. Three Essays, 8vo. 5s.

MOLESWORTH (Mrs.).—MARRYING AND GIVING IN MARRIAGE: a Novel. Fcp. 8vo. 2s. 6d.

——— SILVERTHORNS. With Illustrations by F. Noel Paton. Cr. 8vo. 5s.

——— THE PALACE IN THE GARDEN. With Illustrations. Cr. 8vo. 5s.

——— THE THIRD MISS ST. QUENTIN. Crown 8vo. 6s.

——— NEIGHBOURS. With Illustrations by M. Ellen Edwards. Cr. 8vo. 6s.

——— THE STORY OF A SPRING MORNING. With Illustrations. Cr.8vo. 5s.

MOORE (Edward).—DANTE AND HIS EARLY BIOGRAPHERS. Crown 8vo. 4s. 6d.

MULHALL (Michael G.).—HISTORY OF PRICES SINCE THE YEAR 1850. Crown 8vo. 6s.

MURRAY (David Christie and Henry).—A DANGEROUS CATS-PAW : a Story. Crown 8vo. 2s. 6d.

MURRAY (Christie) and HERMAN (Henry).—WILD DARRIE : a Story. Crown 8vo. 2s. boards ; 2s. 6d. cloth.

NANSEN (Dr. Fridtjof).—THE FIRST CROSSING OF GREENLAND. With 5 Maps, 12 Plates, and 150 Illustrations in the Text. 2 vols. 8vo. 36s.

NAPIER.—THE LIFE OF SIR JOSEPH NAPIER, BART., EX-LORD CHANCELLOR OF IRELAND. By ALEX. CHARLES EWALD. 8vo. 15s.

——— THE LECTURES, ESSAYS, AND LETTERS OF THE RIGHT HON. SIR JOSEPH NAPIER, BART. 8vo. 12s. 6d.

NESBIT (E.).—LEAVES OF LIFE : Verses. Crown 8vo. 5s.

NEWMAN.—THE LETTERS AND CORRESPONDENCE OF JOHN HENRY NEWMAN during his Life in the English Church. With a brief Autobiographical Memoir. Edited by Anne Mozley. With Portraits, 2 vols. 8vo. 30s. *net.*

NEWMAN (Cardinal).—Works by :—

Sermons to Mixed Congregations. Crown 8vo. 6s.

Sermons on Various Occasions. Cr. 8vo. 6s.

The Idea of a University defined and illustrated. Cabinet Edition, Cr. 8vo. 7s. Cheap Edition, Cr. 8vo. 3s. 6d.

Historical Sketches. Cabinet Edition, 3 vols. Crown 8vo 6s. each. Cheap Edition, 3 vols. Cr. 8vo. 3s. 6d. each.

The Arians of the Fourth Century. Cabinet Edition, Crown 8vo. 6s. Cheap Edition, Crown 8vo. 3s. 6d.

Select Treatises of St. Athanasius in Controversy with the Arians. Freely Translated. 2 vols. Cr. 8vo. 15s.

Discussions and Arguments on Various Subjects. Cabinet Edition, Crown 8vo. 6s. Cheap Edition, Crown 8vo. 3s. 6d.

[Continued.

NEWMAN (Cardinal).—Works by :—(continued).

Apologia Pro Vita Sua. Cabinet Ed., Crown 8vo. 6s.   Cheap Ed. 3s. 6d.

Development of Christian Doctrine. Cabinet Edition, Crown 8vo. 6s. Cheap Edition, Cr. 8vo. 3s. 6d.

Certain Difficulties felt by Anglicans in Catholic Teaching Considered. Cabinet Edition. Vol. I. Crown 8vo. 7s. 6d. ; Vol. II. Crown 8vo. 5s. 6d. Cheap Edition, 2 vols. Crown 8vo. 3s. 6d. each.

The Via Media of the Anglican Church, Illustrated in Lectures, &c. Cabinet Edition, 2 vols. Cr. 8vo. 6s. each. Cheap Edition, 2 vols. Crown 8vo. 3s. 6d. each.

Essays, Critical and Historical. Cabinet Edition, 2 vols. Crown 8vo. 12s. Cheap Edition, 2 vols. Cr. 8vo. 7s.

Biblical and Ecclesiastical Miracles. Cabinet Edition, Crown 8vo. 6s. Cheap Edition, Crown 8vo. 3s. 6d.

Present Position of Catholics in England. Crown 8vo. 7s. 6d.

Tracts. 1. Dissertatiunculæ. 2. On the Text of the Seven Epistles of St. Ignatius. 3. Doctrinal Causes of Arianism. 4. Apollinarianism. 5. St. Cyril's Formula. 6. Ordo de Tempore. 7. Douay Version of Scripture. Crown 8vo. 8s.

An Essay in Aid of a Grammar of Assent. Cabinet Edition, Crown 8vo. 7s. 6d. Cheap Edition, Crown 8vo. 3s. 6d.

Callista : a Tale of the Third Century. Cabinet Edition, Crown 8vo. 6s. Cheap Edition, Crown 8vo. 3s. 6d.

Loss and Gain : a Tale. Cabinet Edition, Crown 8vo. 6s. Cheap Edition, Crown 8vo. 3s. 6d.

The Dream of Gerontius. 16mo. 6d. sewed, 1s. cloth.

Verses on Various Occasions. Cabinet Edition, Crown 8vo. 6s. Cheap Edition, Crown 8vo. 3s. 6d.

*** *For Cardinal Newman's other Works see Messrs. Longmans & Co.'s Catalogue of Theological Works.*

NORRIS (W. E.).—MRS. FENTON : a Sketch. Crown 8vo. 6s.

NORTON (Charles L.).—POLITICAL AMERICANISMS : a Glossary of Terms and Phrases Current in American Politics. Crown 8vo. 2s. 6d.

———— A HANDBOOK OF FLORIDA. 49 Maps and Plans. Fcp. 8vo. 5s.

NORTHCOTE (W. H.).—LATHES AND TURNING, Simple, Mechanical, and Ornamental. With 338 Illustrations. 8vo. 18s.

O'BRIEN (William).—WHEN WE WERE BOYS : A Novel. Cr. 8vo, 2s. 6d.

OLIPHANT (Mrs.).—MADAM. Crown 8vo. 1s. boards ; 1s. 6d. cloth.

———— IN TRUST. Crown 8vo. 1s. boards ; 1s. 6d. cloth.

———— LADY CAR : the Sequel of a Life. Crown 8vo. 2s. 6d.

OMAN (C. W. C.).—A HISTORY OF GREECE FROM THE EARLIEST TIMES TO THE MACEDONIAN CONQUEST. With Maps. Cr. 8vo. 4s. 6d.

O'REILLY (Mrs.).—HURSTLEIGH DENE : a Tale. Crown 8vo. 5s.

PAUL (Hermann).—PRINCIPLES OF THE HISTORY OF LANGUAGE. Translated by H. A. Strong. 8vo. 10s. 6d.

PAYN (James).—THE LUCK OF THE DARRELLS. Cr. 8vo. 1s. bds. ; 1s. 6d. cl.

———— THICKER THAN WATER. Crown 8vo. 1s. boards ; 1s. 6d. cloth.

PERRING (Sir Philip).—HARD KNOTS IN SHAKESPEARE. 8vo. 7s. 6d.

———— THE 'WORKS AND DAYS' OF MOSES. Crown 8vo. 3s. 6d.

PHILLIPPS-WOLLEY (C.).—SNAP : a Legend of the Lone Mountain. With 13 Illustrations by H. G. Willink. Crown 8vo. 6s.

POLE (W.).—THE THEORY OF THE MODERN SCIENTIFIC GAME OF WHIST. Fcp. 8vo. 2s. 6d.

POLLOCK (W. H. and Lady).—THE SEAL OF FATE. Cr. 8vo. 6s.

POOLE (W. H. and Mrs.).—COOKERY FOR THE DIABETIC. Fcp. 8vo. 2s. 6d.

PRENDERGAST (John P.).—IRELAND, FROM THE RESTORATION TO THE REVOLUTION, 1660-1690. 8vo. 5s.

PROCTOR (R.A.).—Works by :—

Old and New Astronomy. 12 Parts, 2s. 6d. each. Supplementary Section, 1s. Complete in 1 vol. 4to. 36s. [*In course of publication.*

The Orbs Around Us. Crown 8vo. 5s.

Other Worlds than Ours. With 14 Illustrations. Crown 8vo. 5s.

The Moon. Crown 8vo. 5s.

Universe of Stars. 8vo. 10s. 6d.

Larger Star Atlas for the Library, in 12 Circular Maps, with Introduction and 2 Index Pages. Folio, 15s. or Maps only, 12s. 6d.

The Student's Atlas. In 12 Circular Maps. 8vo. 5s.

New Star Atlas. In 12 Circular Maps. Crown 8vo. 5s.

Light Science for Leisure Hours. 3 vols. Crown 8vo. 5s. each.

Chance and Luck. Crown 8vo. 2s. boards ; 2s. 6d. cloth.

Pleasant Ways in Science. Cr. 8vo. 5s.

How to Play Whist: with the Laws and Etiquette of Whist. Crown 8vo. 3s.6d.

Home Whist: an Easy Guide to Correct Play. 16mo. 1s.

Studies of Venus-Transits. With 7 Diagrams and 10 Plates. 8vo. 5s.

The Stars in their Season. 12 Maps. Royal 8vo. 5s.

Star Primer. Showing the Starry Sky Week by Week, in 24 Hourly Maps. Crown 4to. 2s. 6d.

The Seasons Pictured in 48 Sun-Views of the Earth, and 24 Zodiacal Maps, &c. Demy 4to. 5s.

Strength and Happiness. With 9 Illustrations. Crown 8vo. 5s.

Strength: How to get Strong and keep Strong. Crown 8vo. 2s.

Rough Ways Made Smooth. Essays on Scientific Subjects. Crown 8vo. 5s.

Our Place among Infinities. Cr. 8vo. 5s.

The Expanse of Heaven. Cr. 8vo. 5s.

The Great Pyramid. Crown 8vo. 5s.

Myths and Marvels of Astronomy Crown 8vo. 5s.

Nature Studies. By Grant Allen, A. Wilson, T. Foster, E. Clodd, and R. A. Proctor. Crown 8vo. 5s.

Leisure Readings. By E. Clodd, A. Wilson, T. Foster, A. C. Ranyard, and R. A. Proctor. Crown 8vo. 5s.

PRYCE (John).—THE ANCIENT BRITISH CHURCH : an Historical Essay. Crown 8vo. 6s.

RANSOME (Cyril).—THE RISE OF CONSTITUTIONAL GOVERNMENT IN ENGLAND : being a Series of Twenty Lectures. Crown 8vo. 6s.

RAWLINSON (Canon G.).—THE HISTORY OF PHŒNICIA. 8vo. 24s.

RENDLE (William) and NORMAN (Philip).—THE INNS OF OLD SOUTHWARK, and their Associations. With Illustrations. Royal 8vo. 28s.

RIBOT (Th.).—THE PSYCHOLOGY OF ATTENTION. Crown 8vo. 3s.

RICH (A.).—A DICTIONARY OF ROMAN AND GREEK ANTIQUITIES. With 2000 Woodcuts. Crown 8vo. 7s. 6d.

RICHARDSON (Dr. B. W.).—NATIONAL HEALTH. A Review of the Works of Sir Edwin Chadwick, K.C.B. Crown 4s. 6d.

RILEY (Athelstan).—ATHOS; or, The Mountain of the Monks. With Map and 29 Illustrations. 8vo. 21s.

ROBERTS (Alexander).—GREEK THE LANGUAGE OF CHRIST AND HIS APOSTLES. 8vo. 18s.

ROCKHILL (W. W.).—THE LAND OF THE LAMAS: Notes of a Journey through China, Mongolia, and Tibet. With Maps and Illustrations. 8vo. 15s.

ROGET (John Lewis).—A HISTORY OF THE 'OLD WATER COLOUR' SOCIETY. 2 vols. Royal 8vo. 42s.

ROGET (Peter M.).—THESAURUS OF ENGLISH WORDS AND PHRASES. Crown 8vo. 10s. 6d.

RONALDS (Alfred).—THE FLY-FISHER'S ETYMOLOGY. With 20 Coloured Plates. 8vo. 14s.

ROSSETTI (Maria Francesca).—A SHADOW OF DANTE: being an Essay towards studying Himself, his World, and his Pilgrimage. Cr. 8vo. 10s. 6d.

RUSSELL.—A LIFE OF LORD JOHN RUSSELL. By SPENCER WALPOLE. 2 vols. 8vo. 36s. Cabinet Edition, 2 vols. Crown 8vo. 12s.

SEEBOHM (Frederick). — THE OXFORD REFORMERS — JOHN COLET, ERASMUS, AND THOMAS MORE. 8vo. 14s.

———— THE ENGLISH VILLAGE COMMUNITY Examined in its Relations to the Manorial and Tribal Systems, &c. 13 Maps and Plates. 8vo. 16s.

———— THE ERA OF THE PROTESTANT REVOLUTION. With Map. Fcp. 8vo. 2s. 6d.

SEWELL (Elizabeth M.).—STORIES AND TALES. Crown 8vo. 1s. 6d. each, cloth plain; 2s. 6d. each, cloth extra, gilt edges:—

Amy Herbert.	Katharine Ashton.	Gertrude.
The Earl's Daughter.	Margaret Percival.	Ivors.
The Experience of Life.	Laneton Parsonage.	Home Life.
A Glimpse of the World.	Ursula.	After Life.
Cleve Hall.		

SHAKESPEARE.—BOWDLER'S FAMILY SHAKESPEARE. 1 vol. 8vo. With 36 Woodcuts, 14s., or in 6 vols. Fcp. 8vo. 21s.

———— OUTLINE OF THE LIFE OF SHAKESPEARE. By J. O. HALLIWELL-PHILLIPPS. 2 vols. Royal 8vo. £1 1s.

———— SHAKESPEARE'S TRUE LIFE. By JAMES WALTER. With 500 Illustrations. Imp. 8vo. 21s.

———— THE SHAKESPEARE BIRTHDAY BOOK. By MARY F. DUNBAR. 32mo. 1s. 6d. cloth. With Photographs, 32mo. 5s. Drawing-Room Edition, with Photographs, Fcp. 8vo. 10s. 6d.

SHORT (T. V.).—SKETCH OF THE HISTORY OF THE CHURCH OF ENGLAND to the Revolution of 1688. Crown 8vo. 7s. 6d.

SILVER LIBRARY, The.—Crown 8vo. price 3*s.* 6*d.* each volume.

BAKER'S (Sir S. W.) Eight Years in Ceylon. With 6 Illustrations.

———— **Rifle and Hound in Ceylon.** With 6 Illustrations.

BRASSEY'S (Lady) A Voyage in the 'Sunbeam '. With 66 Illustrations.

CLODD'S (E.) Story of Creation : a Plain Account of Evolution. With 77 Illustrations.

DOYLE'S (A. Conan) Micah Clarke : a Tale of Monmouth's Rebellion.

FROUDE'S (J. A.) Short Studies on Great Subjects. 4 vols.

———— **Cæsar :** a Sketch.

———— **Thomas Carlyle :** a History of his Life. 1795-1835. 2 vols. 1834-1881. 2 vols.

———— **The Two Chiefs of Dunboy :** an Irish Romance of the Last Century.

GLEIG'S (Rev. G. R.) Life of the Duke of Wellington. With Portrait.

HAGGARD'S (H. R.) She : A History of Adventure. 32 Illustrations.

———— **Allan Quatermain.** With 20 Illustrations.

———— **Colonel Quaritch, V.C. :** a Tale of Country Life.

———— **Cleopatra.** With 29 Full-page Illustrations.

HOWITT'S (W.) Visits to Remarkable Places. 80 Illustrations.

JEFFERIES' (R.) The Story of My Heart : My Autobiography. With Portrait.

———— **Field and Hedgerow.** Last Essays of. With Portrait.

MACLEOD'S (H. D.) The Elements of Banking.

MARSHMAN'S (J. C.) Memoirs of Sir Henry Havelock.

MERIVALE'S (Dean) History of the Romans under the Empire. 8 vols.

MILL'S (J. S.) Principles of Political Economy.

———— **System of Logic.**

NEWMAN'S (Cardinal) Historical Sketches. 3 vols.

———— **Apologia Pro Vita Sua.**

———— **Callista :** a Tale of the Third Century.

———— **Loss and Gain :** a Tale.

———— **Essays, Critical and Historical.** 2 vols.

———— **An Essay on the Development of Christian Doctrine.**

———— **The Arians of the Fourth Century.**

———— **Verses on Various Occasions.**

———— **Parochial and Plain Sermons.** 8 vols.

———— **Selection, adapted to the Seasons of the Ecclesiastical Year,** from the ' Parochial and Plain Sermons '.

———— **Difficulties felt by Anglicans in Catholic Teaching Considered.** 2 vols.

———— **The Idea of a University** defined and Illustrated.

———— **Biblical and Ecclesiastical Miracles.**

———— **Discussions and Arguments on Various Subjects.**

———— **Grammar of Assent.**

———— **The Via Media of the Anglican Church,** illustrated in Lectures, &c. 2 vols.

———— **Sermons bearing upon Subjects of the Day.** Edited by the Rev. J. W. Copeland, B.D., late Rector of Farnham, Essex.

STANLEY'S (Bishop) Familiar History of Birds. With 160 Illustrations.

WOOD'S (Rev. J. G.) Petland Revisited. With 33 Illustrations.

———— **Strange Dwellings.** With 60 Illustrations.

———— **Out of Doors.** With 11 Illustrations.

SMITH (R. Bosworth).—CARTHAGE AND THE CARTHAGINIANS. Maps, Plans, &c.   Crown 8vo. 6s.

SOPHOCLES.   Translated into English Verse.   By ROBERT WHITELAW. Crown 8vo. 8s. 6d.

STANLEY (E.).—A FAMILIAR HISTORY OF BIRDS.   With 160 Woodcuts.   Crown 8vo. 3s. 6d

STEEL (J. H.).—A TREATISE ON THE DISEASES OF THE DOG; being a Manual of Canine Pathology.   88 Illustrations.   8vo. 10s. 6d.

———— A TREATISE ON THE DISEASES OF THE OX ; being a Manual of Bovine Pathology.   2 Plates and 117 Woodcuts.   8vo. 15s.

———— A TREATISE ON THE DISEASES OF THE SHEEP; being a Manual of Ovine Pathology.   With Coloured Plate and 99 Woodcuts.   8vo. 12s.'

STEPHEN (Sir James).—ESSAYS IN ECCLESIASTICAL BIOGRAPHY.   Crown 8vo. 7s. 6d.

STEPHENS (H. Morse).—A HISTORY OF THE FRENCH REVOLUTION.   3 vols. 8vo.   Vol. I. 18s.   Vol. II. 18s.   [*Vol. III. in the press.*

STEVENSON (Robt. Louis).—A CHILD'S GARDEN OF VERSES. Small Fcp. 8vo. 5s.

———— THE DYNAMITER.   Fcp. 8vo. 1s. sewed, 1s. 6d. cloth.

———— STRANGE CASE OF DR. JEKYLL AND MR. HYDE.   Fcp. 8vo. 1s. sewed, 1s. 6d. cloth.

STEVENSON (Robert Louis) and OSBOURNE (Lloyd).—THE WRONG BOX.   Crown 8vo. 5s.

STOCK (St. George).—DEDUCTIVE LOGIC.   Fcp. 8vo. 3s. 6d.

'STONEHENGE.'—THE DOG IN HEALTH AND DISEASE.   With 84 Wood Engravings.   Square Crown 8vo. 7s. 6d.

STRONG (Herbert A.), LOGEMAN (Willem S.) and WHEELER (B. I.).—INTRODUCTION TO THE STUDY OF THE HISTORY OF LANGUAGE.   8vo. 10s. 6d.

SUPERNATURAL RELIGION ; an Inquiry into the Reality of Divine Revelation.   3 vols. 8vo. 36s.

REPLY (A) TO DR. LIGHTFOOT'S ESSAYS.   By the Author of 'Supernatural Religion '.   8vo. 6s.

STUTFIELD (H.).—THE BRETHREN OF MOUNT ATLAS: being the First Part of an African Theosophical Story.   Crown 8vo. 6s.

SYMES (J. E.).—PRELUDE TO MODERN HISTORY: being a Brief Sketch of the World's History from the Third to the Ninth Century.   With 5 Maps.   Crown 8vo. 2s. 6d.

TAYLOR (Colonel Meadows).—A STUDENT'S MANUAL OF THE HISTORY OF INDIA, from the Earliest Period to the Present Time.   Crown 8vo. 7s. 6d.

THOMPSON (D. Greenleaf).—THE PROBLEM OF EVIL: an Introduction to the Practical Sciences.   8vo. 10s. 6d.

———— A SYSTEM OF PSYCHOLOGY.   2 vols. 8vo. 36s.

———— THE RELIGIOUS SENTIMENTS OF THE HUMAN MIND.   8vo. 7s. 6d.

———— SOCIAL PROGRESS : an Essay.   8vo. 7s. 6d.

———— THE PHILOSOPHY OF FICTION IN LITERATURE : an Essay. Crown 8vo. 6s.

THREE IN NORWAY. By Two of THEM. With a Map and 59 Illustrations. Crown 8vo. 2s. boards; 2s. 6d. cloth.

TOYNBEE (Arnold).—LECTURES ON THE INDUSTRIAL REVOLUTION OF THE 18th CENTURY IN ENGLAND. 8vo. 10s. 6d.

TREVELYAN (Sir G. O., Bart.).—THE LIFE AND LETTERS OF LORD MACAULAY.

Popular Edition. Crown 8vo. 2s. 6d.	Cabinet Edition, 2 vols. Cr. 8vo. 12s.
Student's Edition. Crown 8vo. 6s.	Library Edition, 2 vols. 8vo. 36s.

———— THE EARLY HISTORY OF CHARLES JAMES FOX. Library Edition, 8vo. 18s. Cabinet Edition, Crown 8vo. 6s.

TROLLOPE (Anthony).—THE WARDEN. Cr. 8vo. 1s. bds., 1s. 6d. cl.

———— BARCHESTER TOWERS. Crown 8vo. 1s. boards, 1s. 6d. cloth.

VILLE (G.).—THE PERPLEXED FARMER: How is he to meet Alien Competition? Crown 8vo. 5s.

VIRGIL. — PUBLI VERGILI MARONIS BUCOLICA, GEORGICA, ÆNEIS; the Works of VIRGIL, Latin Text, with English Commentary and Index. By B. H. KENNEDY. Crown 8vo. 10s. 6d.

———— THE ÆNEID OF VIRGIL. Translated into English Verse. By John Conington. Crown 8vo. 6s.

———— THE POEMS OF VIRGIL. Translated into English Prose. By John Conington. Crown 8vo. 6s.

———— THE ECLOGUES AND GEORGICS OF VIRGIL. Translated from the Latin by J. W. Mackail. Printed on Dutch Hand-made Paper. 16mo. 5s.

WAKEMAN (H. O.) and HASSALL (A.).—ESSAYS INTRODUCTORY TO THE STUDY OF ENGLISH CONSTITUTIONAL HISTORY. Edited by H. O. WAKEMAN and A. HASSALL. Crown 8vo. 6s.

WALKER (A. Campbell-).—THE CORRECT CARD; or, How to Play at Whist; a Whist Catechism. Fcp. 8vo. 2s. 6d.

WALPOLE (Spencer).—HISTORY OF ENGLAND FROM THE CONCLUSION OF THE GREAT WAR IN 1815 to 1858. Library Edition. 5 vols. 8vo. £4 10s. Cabinet Edition. 6 vols. Crown 8vo. 6s. each.

WELLINGTON.—LIFE OF THE DUKE OF WELLINGTON. By the Rev. G. R. GLEIG. Crown 8vo. 3s. 6d.

WENDT (Ernest Emil).—PAPERS ON MARITIME LEGISLATION, with a Translation of the German Mercantile Laws relating to Maritime Commerce. Royal 8vo. £1 11s. 6d.

WEYMAN (Stanley J.).—THE HOUSE OF THE WOLF: a Romance. Crown 8vo. 6s.

WHATELY (E. Jane).—ENGLISH SYNONYMS. Edited by Archbishop WHATELY. Fcp. 8vo. 3s.

———— LIFE AND CORRESPONDENCE OF ARCHBISHOP WHATELY. With Portrait. Crown 8vo. 10s. 6d.

WHATELY (Archbishop).—ELEMENTS OF LOGIC. Cr. 8vo. 4s. 6d.

———— ELEMENTS OF RHETORIC. Crown 8vo. 4s. 6d.

———— LESSONS ON REASONING. Fcp. 8vo. 1s. 6d.

———— BACON'S ESSAYS, with Annotations. 8vo. 10s. 6d.

WILCOCKS (J. C.).—THE SEA FISHERMAN. Comprising the Chief Methods of Hook and Line Fishing in the British and other Seas, and Remarks on Nets, Boats, and Boating. Profusely Illustrated. Crown 8vo. 6s.

WILLICH (Charles M.).—POPULAR TABLES for giving Information for ascertaining the value of Lifehold, Leasehold, and Church Property, the Public Funds, &c. Edited by H. BENCE JONES. Crown 8vo. 10s. 6d.

WILLOUGHBY (Captain Sir John C.).—EAST AFRICA AND ITS BIG GAME. Illustrated by G. D. Giles and Mrs. Gordon Hake. Royal 8vo. 21s.

WITT (Prof.)—Works by. Translated by Frances Younghusband.

———— THE TROJAN WAR. Crown 8vo. 2s.

———— MYTHS OF HELLAS; or, Greek Tales. Crown 8vo. 3s. 6d.

———— THE WANDERINGS OF ULYSSES. Crown 8vo. 3s. 6d.

———— THE RETREAT OF THE TEN THOUSAND; being the Story of Xenophon's 'Anabasis'. With Illustrations. Crown 8vo. 3s. 6d.

WOLFF (Henry W.).—RAMBLES IN THE BLACK FOREST. Crown 8vo. 7s. 6d.

———— THE WATERING PLACES OF THE VOSGES. With Map. Crown 8vo. 4s. 6d.

———— THE COUNTRY OF THE VOSGES. With a Map. 8vo. 12s.

WOOD (Rev. J. G.).—HOMES WITHOUT HANDS; a Description of the Habitations of Animals. With 140 Illustrations. 8vo. 10s. 6d.

———— INSECTS AT HOME; a Popular Account of British Insects, their Structure, Habits, and Transformations. With 700 Illustrations. 8vo. 10s. 6d.

———— INSECTS ABROAD; a Popular Account of Foreign Insects, their Structure, Habits, and Transformations. With 600 Illustrations. 8vo. 10s. 6d.

———— BIBLE ANIMALS; a Description of every Living Creature mentioned in the Scriptures. With 112 Illustrations. 8vo. 10s. 6d.

———— STRANGE DWELLINGS; abridged from 'Homes without Hands'. With 60 Illustrations. Crown 8vo. 3s. 6d.

———— OUT OF DOORS; a Selection of Original Articles on Practical Natural History. With 11 Illustrations. Crown 8vo. 3s. 6d.

———— PETLAND REVISITED. With 33 Illustrations. Crown 8vo. 3s. 6d.

WORDSWORTH (Bishop Charles).—ANNALS OF MY EARLY LIFE, 1806-1846. 8vo. 15s.

WYLIE (J. H.).—HISTORY OF ENGLAND UNDER HENRY THE FOURTH. Crown 8vo. Vol. I. 10s. 6d. ; Vol. II.

YOUATT (William).—THE HORSE. With numerous Woodcuts. 8vo. 7s. 6d.

———— THE DOG. With numerous Woodcuts. 8vo. 6s.

ZELLER (Dr. E.).—HISTORY OF ECLECTICISM IN GREEK PHILO-SOPHY. Translated by Sarah F. Alleyne. Crown 8vo. 10s. 6d.

———— THE STOICS, EPICUREANS, AND SCEPTICS. Translated by the Rev. O. J. Reichel. Crown 8vo. 15s.

———— SOCRATES AND THE SOCRATIC SCHOOLS. Translated by the Rev. O. J. Reichel. Crown 8vo. 10s. 6d.

———— PLATO AND THE OLDER ACADEMY. Translated by Sarah F. Alleyne and Alfred Goodwin. Crown 8vo. 18s.

———— THE PRE-SOCRATIC SCHOOLS. Translated by Sarah F. Alleyne. 2 vols. Crown 8vo. 30s.

———— OUTLINES OF THE HISTORY OF GREEK PHILOSOPHY. Translated by Sarah F. Alleyne and Evelyn Abbott. Crown 8vo. 10s. 6d.

50,000—10/91. ABERDEEN UNIVERSITY PRESS.

Printed in Great Britain
by Amazon